A MIDSUMMER NIGHT'S DREAM

WITH READER'S GUIDE

AMSCO LITERATURE PROGRAM

William Shakespeare

A MIDSUMMER NIGHT'S DREAM

Amsco Literature Program

When ordering this book, you may specify:
R 511 ALP *(Paperback)*
R 511 H *(Hardbound)*

WITH READER'S GUIDE

Abraham Ponemon

Amsco School Publications, Inc.
315 HUDSON STREET NEW YORK, N.Y. 10013

ISBN 0-87720-923-5 (Paperback)
ISBN 0-87720-924-3 (Hardbound)

A Midsummer Night's Dream with Reader's Guide

Printed in the United States of America

CONTENTS

Characters in the Play

Theseus, Duke of Athens
Egeus, father to Hermia
Lysander ⎫
Demetrius ⎭ in love with Hermia

Philostrate, Master of the Revels to Theseus
Peter Quince, a carpenter
Nick Bottom, a weaver
Francis Flute, a bellows-mender
Tom Snout, a tinker
Snug, a joiner
Robin Starveling, a tailor

Hippolyta, Queen of the Amazons, betrothed to Theseus
Hermia, daughter to Egeus, in love with Lysander
Helena, in love with Demetrius

Oberon, King of the Fairies
Titania, Queen of the Fairies
Puck, or Robin Goodfellow

Peaseblossom ⎫
Cobweb ⎪
Moth ⎬ fairies
Mustardseed ⎭

Other *fairies* attending Oberon and Titania
Attendants on Theseus and Hippolyta

SCENE: Athens, and a nearby wood

A Midsummer Night's Dream

1 **nuptial** marriage
2 **apace** quickly

4 **lingers** slows the fulfillment of

6 **withering out** diminishing

7 **steep themselves** become absorbed

11 **solemnities** marriage rites

14 **pert** vivacious; lively

16 **pale companion** colorless fellow
   pomp brilliant display

20 **triumph** public show of victory
   reveling having a wild celebration

ACT I

Enter Theseus, Hippolyta, Philostrate, and Attendants.

Theseus
    Now, fair Hippolyta, our nuptial hour
    Draws on apace. Four happy days bring in
    Another moon. But, O, methinks, how slow
    This old moon wanes! She lingers my desires,
    Like to a step-dame, or a dowager,   5
    Long withering out a young man's revenue.
Hippolyta
    Four days will quickly steep themselves in night.
    Four nights will quickly dream away the time;
    And then the moon, like to a silver bow
    New-bent in heaven, shall behold the night   10
    Of our solemnities.
Theseus
                Go, Philostrate,
    Stir up the Athenian youth to merriments.
    Awake the pert and nimble spirit of mirth,
    Turn melancholy forth to funerals;   15
    The pale companion is not for our pomp.
                     [*Exit Philostrate.*
    Hippolyta, I woo'd thee with my sword,
    And won thy love, doing thee injuries;
    But I will wed thee in another key,
    With pomp, with triumph, and with reveling.   20

    Enter Egeus, Hermia, Lysander, and Demetrius.

23 **vexation** affliction; irritation; troubled mind

28 **bosom** considered the seat of one's emotions
29 **rhymes** love poems

32 **feigning** false; deceptive
33 **stolen . . . fantasy** made her fall in love with you
34 **gawds** jewels
   conceits showy trinkets
35 **knacks; nosegays; sweetmeats** trivial gifts; posies; can-
   dies
36 **prevailment** persuasiveness
   unharden'd easily impressed

40 **Be it so** if it is a fact that

42 **ancient privilege of Athens** the legal right of an Athenian father to dictate whom his daughter may marry

46 **Immediately** specifically; expressly

49 **composed** created (through fatherhood)
50 **form** impression

52 **leave; figure; disfigure** allow; image; destroy
53 **worthy** noble

Egeus
  Happy be Theseus, our renowned duke!
Theseus
  Thanks, good Egeus. What's the news with thee?
Egeus
  Full of vexation come I, with complaint
  Against my child, my daughter Hermia.
  Stand forth, Demetrius. My noble lord,   25
  This man hath my consent to marry her.
  Stand forth, Lysander. And, my gracious duke,
  This man hath bewitch'd the bosom of my child.
  Thou, thou, Lysander, thou hast given her rhymes,
  And interchanged love-tokens with my child.   30
  Thou hast by moonlight at her window sung,
  With feigning voice, verses of feigning love,
  And stolen the impression of her fantasy
  With bracelets of thy hair, rings, gawds, conceits,
  Knacks, trifles, nosegays, sweetmeats, messengers   35
  Of strong prevailment in unharden'd youth.
  With cunning hast thou filch'd my daughter's heart,
  Turn'd her obedience, which is due to me,
  To stubborn harshness. And, my gracious duke,
  Be it so she will not here before your Grace   40
  Consent to marry with Demetrius,
  I beg the ancient privilege of Athens.
  As she is mine, I may dispose of her,
  Which shall be either to this gentleman
  Or to her death, according to our law   45
  Immediately provided in that case.
Theseus
  What say you, Hermia? Be advised, fair maid.
  To you your father should be as a god,
  One that composed your beauties; yea, and one
  To whom you are but as a form in wax   50
  By him imprinted and within his power
  To leave the figure or disfigure it.
  Demetrius is a worthy gentleman.

56 **kind** respect
   voice consent

62 **how . . . modesty** whether it is consistent with mod-
   est behavior
63 **to plead my thoughts** to express my own opinion

67 **die the death** to be put to death by the sentence of
   a judge
   adjure renounce
70 **Know of your youth** learn by questioning your youth-
   ful feelings
   blood passions
72 **livery** clothing
73 **aye** forever
   mew'd confined
75 **faint** low-voiced and lacking emotions
   moon Diana, the virgin goddess
76 **master their blood** repress their natural desires
77 **maiden pilgrimage** life's journey as a virgin
78 **rose distill'd** roses were distilled to make perfume
80 **single blessedness** holy blessing given to one living
   an unmarried life

82 **virgin patent** privilege of remaining a virgin

Hermia
So is Lysander.
Theseus
    In himself he is;   55
But in this kind, wanting your father's voice,
The other must be held the worthier.
Hermia
I would my father look'd but with my eyes.
Theseus
Rather your eyes must with his judgment look.
Hermia
I do entreat your Grace to pardon me.   60
I know not by what power I am made bold,
Nor how it may concern my modesty,
In such a presence here to plead my thoughts.
But I beseech your Grace that I may know
The worst that may befall me in this case, 65
If I refuse to wed Demetrius.
Theseus
Either to die the death, or to adjure
Forever the society of men.
Therefore, fair Hermia, question your desires.
Know of your youth, examine well your blood, 70
Whether, if you yield not to your father's choice,
You can endure the livery of a nun,
For aye to be in shady cloister mew'd,
To live a barren sister all your life,
Chanting faint hymns to the cold fruitless moon. 75
Thrice-blessed they that master so their blood,
To undergo such maiden pilgrimage;
But earthlier happy is the rose distill'd,
Than that which, withering on the virgin thorn,
Grows, lives, and dies in single blessedness. 80
Hermia
So will I grow, so live, so die, my lord,
Ere I will yield my virgin patent up

91 **protest** vow
92 **austerity** devotion to the disciplined life of a nun

94 **crazed** flawed

100 **estate unto** bestow upon; settle; convey

101 **well derived** well born
102 **well possess'd** well off

104 **with vantage** better

106 **of** by

108 **avouch** affirm
head face

112 **spotted** treacherous

Unto his lordship, whose unwished yoke
My soul consents not to give sovereignty.

Theseus

Take time to pause; and, by the next new moon—   85
The sealing-day betwixt my love and me,
For everlasting bond of fellowship—
Upon that day either prepare to die
For disobedience to your father's will,
Or else to wed Demetrius, as he would,   90
Or on Diana's altar to protest
For aye austerity and single life.

Demetrius

Relent, sweet Hermia! And, Lysander, yield
Thy crazed title to my certain right

Lysander

You have her father's love, Demetrius,   95
Let me have Hermia's. Do you marry him.

Egeus

Scornful Lysander! True, he hath my love,
And what is mine my love shall render him.
And she is mine, and all my right of her
I do estate unto Demetrius.   100

Lysander

I am, my lord, as well derived as he,
As well possess'd; my love is more than his;
My fortunes every way as fairly rank'd,
If not with vantage, as Demetrius'.
And, which is more than all these boasts can be,   105
I am beloved of beauteous Hermia.
Why should not I then prosecute my right?
Demetrius, I'll avouch it to his head,
Made love to Nedar's daughter, Helena,
And won her soul; and she, sweet lady, dotes,   110
Devoutly dotes, dotes in idolatry,
Upon this spotted and inconstant man.

Theseus

I must confess that I have heard so much,

116 **mind**   memory

118 **schooling**   advice
119 **arm yourself**   make up your mind
120 **fancies**   thoughts of love

122 **extenuate**   weaken

128 **nearly**   closely

129 **duty and desire**   eagerness to serve

132 **Belike**   probably
133 **Beteem**   allow
     tempest   storm of tears

137 **blood**   inherited rank

138 **cross!**   bad luck!

139 **misgraffed**   ill-matched

141 **stood**   was based
     friends   relatives

And with Demetrius thought to have spoke thereof;
But, being over-full of self-affairs,   115
My mind did lose it. But, Demetrius, come;
And come, Egeus. You shall go with me.
I have some private schooling for you both.
For you, fair Hermia, look you arm yourself
To fit your fancies to your father's will;   120
Or else the law of Athens yields you up—
Which by no means we may extenuate—
To death, or to a vow of single life.
Come, my Hippolyta. What cheer, my love?
Demetrius and Egeus, go along.   125
I must employ you in some business
Against our nuptial, and confer with you
Of something nearly that concerns yourselves.

Egeus
With duty and desire we follow you.
              [*Exeunt all but Lysander and Hermia.*

Lysander
How now, my love! Why is your cheek so pale?   130
How chance the roses there do fade so fast?

Hermia
Belike for want of rain, which I could well
Beteem them from the tempest of my eyes.

Lysander
Aye me! For aught that I could ever read,
Could ever hear by tale or history,   135
The course of true love never did run smooth;
But, either it was different in blood—

Hermia
O cross! Too high to be enthrall'd to low!

Lysander
Or else misgraffed in respect of years—

Hermia
O spite! Too old to be engaged to young!   140

Lysander
Or else it stood upon the choice of friends—

143 **sympathy** harmony

147 **collied** dark
148 **in a spleen** on a moment's impulse

151 **confusion** destruction

152 **ever cross'd** always frustrated

154 **teach . . . patience** let us discipline ourselves to accept our fate patiently
156 **thoughts** fits of melancholy

158 **A good persuasion** a sound doctrine
159 **dowager** a widow with property

162 **respects** regards

169 **do . . . May** celebrate May Day
170 **stay** wait

173 **best arrow** Cupid's gold-tipped arrow brings love; his
blunt, leaden-tipped arrow produces aversion

Hermia
  O hell! To choose love by another's eyes!
Lysander
  Or, if there were a sympathy in choice,
  War, death, or sickness did lay siege to it
  Making it momentary as a sound,   145
  Swift as a shadow, short as any dream,
  Brief as the lightning in the collied night,
  That, in a spleen, unfolds both heaven and earth,
  And ere a man hath power to say 'Behold!'
  The jaws of darkness do devour it up.   150
  So quick bright things come to confusion.
Hermia
  If then true lovers have been ever cross'd,
  It stands as an edict in destiny.
  Then let us teach our trial patience,
  Because it is a customary cross,   155
  As due to love as thoughts and dreams and sighs,
  Wishes and tears, poor fancy's followers.
Lysander
  A good persuasion. Therefore, hear me, Hermia.
  I have a widow aunt, a dowager
  Of great revenue, and she hath no child.   160
  From Athens is her house remote seven leagues,
  And she respects me as her only son.
  There, gentle Hermia, may I marry thee,
  And to that place the sharp Athenian law
  Cannot pursue us. If thou lovest me, then,   165
  Steal forth thy father's house tomorrow night;
  And in the wood, a league without the town,
  Where I did meet thee once with Helena,
  To do observance to a morn of May,
  There will I stay for thee.   170
Hermia
                    My good Lysander!
  I swear to thee, by Cupid's strongest bow,
  By his best arrow with the golden head,

176 **Carthage queen** Dido (in the Aeneid) burned herself on a funeral pyre after her Trojan lover Aeneas left her

183 **speed** prosper

184 **fair** beautiful
185 **your fair** your blond beauty
186 **lodestars** the bright pole star guiding voyagers
   air music

189 **favor** features

193 **bated** excepted
194 **translated** transformed

196 **motion** inclination

200 **move** arouse

By the simplicity of Venus' doves,
By that which knitteth souls and prospers loves,   175
And by that fire which burn'd the Carthage queen,
When the false Troyan under sail was seen,
By all the vows that ever men have broke,
In number more than ever women spoke,
In that same place thou hast appointed me,   180
Tomorrow truly will I meet with thee.

Lysander
Keep promise, love. Look, here comes Helena.

  Enter Helena.

Hermia
God speed fair Helena! Whither away?

Helena
Call you me fair? That fair again unsay.
Demetrius loves your fair. O happy fair!   185
Your eyes are lodestars, and your tongue's sweet air
More tuneable than lark to shepherd's ear,
When wheat is green, when hawthorn buds appear.
Sickness is catching. O, were favor so,
Yours would I catch, fair Hermia, ere I go.   190
My ear should catch your voice, my eye your eye,
My tongue should catch your tongue's sweet melody.
Were the world mine, Demetrius being bated,
The rest I'ld give to be to you translated.
O, teach me how you look, and with what art   195
You sway the motion of Demetrius' heart!

Hermia
I frown upon him, yet he loves me still.

Helena
O that your frowns would teach my smiles such skill!

Hermia
I give him curses, yet he gives me love.

Helena
O that my prayers could such affection move!   200

Hermia
The more I hate, the more he follows me.

209 **graces** delightful qualities

212 **Phoebe** Diana (the moon)
213 **glass** mirror

215 **still** always

218 **faint** delicately scented
219 **counsel** inmost thought

222 **stranger companies** the company of strangers

225 **starve . . . food** avoid seeing each other

Helena
    The more I love, the more he hateth me.
Hermia
    His folly, Helena, is no fault of mine.
Helena
    None, but your beauty. Would that fault were mine!
Hermia
    Take comfort. He no more shall see my face.   205
    Lysander and myself will fly this place.
    Before the time I did Lysander see,
    Seem'd Athens as a paradise to me.
    O, then, what graces in my love do dwell,
    That he hath turn'd a heaven unto a hell!   210
Lysander
    Helen, to you our minds we will unfold.
    Tomorrow night, when Phœbe doth behold
    Her silver visage in the watery glass,
    Decking with liquid pearl the bladed grass,
    A time that lovers' flights doth still conceal,   215
    Through Athens' gates have we devised to steal.
Hermia
    And in the wood, where often you and I
    Upon faint primrose beds were wont to lie,
    Emptying our bosoms of their counsel sweet,
    There my Lysander and myself shall meet,   220
    And thence from Athens turn away our eyes,
    To seek new friends and stranger companies.
    Farewell, sweet playfellow. Pray thou for us.
    And good luck grant thee thy Demetrius!
    Keep word, Lysander. We must starve our sight   225
    From lovers' food till morrow deep midnight.
Lysander
    I will, my Hermia.
                                      [*Exit Hermia.*
                    Helena, adieu.
    As you on him, Demetrius dote on you!
                                            [*Exit.*

230 **other some**   some others

235 **So I ... qualities**   So I err in admiring his qualities

237 **dignity**   value

240 **taste**   a trace
241 **Wings**   refers to blind Cupid
    figure   symbolize

246 **eyne**   eyes

252 **intelligence**   information

254 **But ... again**   I shall reward myself richly for the pain
    by the joy of seeing him as he leaves and returns

Helena

How happy some o'er other some can be!   230
Through Athens I am thought as fair as she.
But what of that? Demetrius thinks not so.
He will not know what all but he do know.
And as he errs, doting on Hermia's eyes,
So I, admiring of his qualities.   235
Things base and vile, holding no quantity,
Love can transpose to form and dignity.
Love looks not with the eyes, but with the mind,
And therefore is wing'd Cupid painted blind.
Nor hath Love's mind of any judgment taste;   240
Wings, and no eyes, figure unheedy haste.
And therefore is Love said to be a child,
Because in choice he is so oft beguiled.
As waggish boys in game themselves forswear,
So the boy Love is perjured everywhere.   245
For ere Demetrius look'd on Hermia's eyne,
He hail'd down oaths that he was only mine;
And when this hail some heat from Hermia felt,
So he dissolved, and showers of oaths did melt.
I will go tell him of fair Hermia's flight.   250
Then to the wood will he tomorrow night
Pursue her; and for this intelligence
If I have thanks, it is a dear expense.
But herein mean I to enrich my pain,
To have his sight thither and back again.   255

                                        [*Exit.*

2 **generally** individually (a verbal blunder)
3 **scrip** written list

4 **which** who

6 **interlude** short play

9 **on** of
grow to a point conclude

11 **Marry** by the Virgin Mary (an oath) meaning *why, indeed*

15 **spread yourselves** come forth when your name is called

Scene 2. The same. Quince's house

*Enter Quince, Snug, Bottom, Flute, Snout, and
Starveling.*

Quince
Is all our company here?

Bottom
You were best to call them generally, man by man,
according to the scrip.

Quince
Here is the scroll of every man's name, which is
thought fit, through all Athens, to play in our   5
interlude before the duke and the duchess, on his
wedding day at night.

Bottom
First, good Peter Quince, say what the play treats
on. Then read the names of the actors, and so grow
to a point.   10

Quince
Marry, our play is, The most lamentable comedy,
and most cruel death of Pyramus and Thisby.

Bottom
A very good piece of work, I assure you, and a merry.
Now, good Peter Quince, call forth your actors by
the scroll. Masters, spread yourselves.   15

Quince
Answer as I call you. Nick Bottom, the weaver.

Bottom
Ready. Name what part I am for, and proceed.

Quince
You, Nick Bottom, are set down for Pyramus.

Bottom
What is Pyramus? A lover, or a tyrant?

Quince
A lover, that kills himself most gallant for love.   20

22 **look to their eyes** watch out lest they weep too much
23 **condole** show grief
24 **humor** temperamental inclination
25 **part . . . in** a raging part with violent gestures
   to make all split to be very loud and violent in speech
   and action

31 **Phibbus' car** the chariot of Phoebus, the sun god

36 **Ercles'** Hercules'
37 **condoling** able to show grief

41 **What** what sort of man
   wandering knight knight errant

45 **That's all one** that makes no difference
46 **small** high-pitched

47 **An** if

Bottom

That will ask some tears in the true performing of
it. If I do it, let the audience look to their eyes. I will
move storms, I will condole in some measure. To the
rest: yet my chief humor is for a tyrant. I could play
Ercles rarely, or a part to tear a cat in, to make all   25
split.

> The raging rocks
> And shivering shocks
> Shall break the locks
>   Of prison-gates;   30
> And Phibbus' car
> Shall shine from far,
> And make and mar
>   The foolish Fates.

This was lofty! Now name the rest of the players.   35
This is Ercles' vein, a tyrant's vein. A lover is more
condoling.

Quince

Francis Flute, the bellows mender.

Flute

Here, Peter Quince.

Quince

Flute, you must take Thisby on you.   40

Flute

What is Thisby? A wandering knight?

Quince

It is the lady that Pyramus must love.

Flute

Nay, faith, let not me play a woman. I have a beard
coming.

Quince

That's all one. You shall play it in a mask, and you   45
may speak as small as you will.

Bottom

An I may hide my face, let me play Thisby too, I'll
speak in a monstrous little voice, "Thisne, Thisne."

60 **joiner** furniture maker
61 **fitted** well cast

64 **extempore** without a text

67 **that** so that

70 **terribly** terrifyingly

"Ah Pyramus, my lover dear! Thy Thisby dear, and
lady dear!"   50

Quince
No, no, you must play Pyramus; and, Flute, you
Thisby.

Bottom
Well, proceed.

Quince
Robin Starveling, the tailor.

Starveling
Here, Peter Quince.   55

Quince
Robin Starveling, you must play Thisby's mother.
Tom Snout, the tinker.

Snout
Here, Peter Quince.

Quince
You, Pyramus' father: myself, Thisby's father: Snug,
the joiner; you, the lion's part: and, I hope, here is   60
a play fitted.

Snug
Have you the lion's part written? Pray you, if it be,
give it me, for I am slow of study.

Quince
You may do it extempore, for it is nothing but
roaring.   65

Bottom
Let me play the lion too. I will roar, that I will do
any man's heart good to hear me. I will roar, that I
will make the duke say, "Let him roar again, let him
roar again."

Quince
An you should do it too terribly, you would fright   70
the duchess and the ladies, that they would shriek.
And that were enough to hang us all.

76 **aggravate** moderate (Bottom misuses the word. He means just the opposite of what he says.)

80 **proper** handsome

86 **discharge** perform
87 **purple-in-grain** deep red
88 **French crown color** golden

92 **am to** must
93 **con** learn by heart

97 **devices** dramatic plays
   a bill of properties a list of furnishings for the stage

All

That would hang us, every mother's son.

Bottom

I grant you, friends, if you should fright the ladies
out of their wits, they would have no more discretion   75
but to hang us. But I will aggravate my voice so, that
I will roar you as gently as any sucking dove. I will
roar you an 'twere any nightingale.

Quince

You can play no part but Pyramus, for Pyramus is a
sweet-faced man—a proper man, as one shall see in   80
a summer's day, a most lovely, gentleman-like man.
Therefore you must needs play Pyramus.

Bottom

Well, I will undertake it. What beard were I best to
play it in?

Quince

Why, what you will.   85

Bottom

I will discharge it in either your straw-color beard,
your orange-tawny beard, your purple-in-grain beard,
or your French crown color beard, your perfect
yellow.

Quince

Some of your French crowns have no hair at all, and   90
then you will play barefaced. But, masters, here are
your parts; and I am to entreat you, request you, and
desire you, to con them by tomorrow night, and meet
me in the palace wood, a mile without the town, by
moonlight. There will we rehearse, for if we meet in   95
the city, we shall be dogged with company, and our
devices known. In the meantime I will draw a bill of
properties, such as our play wants. I pray you, fail
me not.

Bottom

We will meet; and there we may rehearse most   100

101 obscenely related to scene. Bottom obviously misuses the word. He may mean *dramatically* or *obscurely*

104 hold . . . strings keep your date or admit you're worthless

obscenely and courageously. Take pains; be perfect.
Adieu.

Quince
At the duke's oak we meet.

Bottom
Enough; hold or cut bowstrings.

[*Exeunt.*

3 **Thorough** through
4 **pale** enclosure; fence

9 **orbs** fairy rings; circles
10 **pensioners** royal bodyguards

12 **favors** jewels; love tokens
13 **savors** perfumes

15 **pearl** gentlemen often wore pearls in their ears
16 **lob** a clumsy person; a country bumpkin
17 **anon** at once

20 **passing fell and wrath** very fierce and angry

ACT II

Scene 1. A wood near Athens

Enter, from opposite sides, a Fairy, and Puck.

Puck
How now, spirit! Whither wander you?
Fairy
    Over hill, over dale,
        Thorough bush, thorough brier,
    Over park, over pale
        Thorough flood, thorough fire,   5
    I do wander everywhere,
    Swifter than the moon's sphere;
    And I serve the fairy queen,
    To dew her orbs upon the green.
    The cowslips tall her pensioners be.   10
    In their gold coats spots you see;
    Those be rubies, fairy favors,
    In those freckles live their savors.
I must go seek some dewdrops here,
And hang a pearl in every cowslip's ear.   15
Farewell, thou lob of spirits, I'll be gone.
Our queen and all her elves come here anon.
Puck
The king doth keep his revels here tonight.
Take heed the queen come not within his sight.
For Oberon is passing fell and wrath,   20
Because that she as her attendant hath
A lovely boy, stolen from an Indian king;

31

23 **changeling** stolen child; people believed fairies kidnapped babies
25 **trace** track
26 **perforce** forcibly

29 **fountain** spring
30 **square** make the posture of fighting without actually fighting; quarrel

32 **making** form
33 **shrewd** mischievous

35 **villagery** village folk; peasantry
36 **Skim milk** Robin steals the cream and interferes with the work of the milkmaids.
  quern hand mill for grinding wheat
37 **bootless** vainly
38 **bear no barm** fail to ferment; go flat

48 **gossip's bowl** a godparent's bowl of liquor
49 **crab** crabapple. These were put in ale to curdle the drink.
51 **dewlap** loose skin around the throat
52 **aunt** old woman

56 **quire** choir; jolly company
57 **waxen (verb)** grow loud
  neeze sneeze

She never had so sweet a changeling.
And jealous Oberon would have the child
Knight of his train, to trace the forests wild.   25
But she perforce withholds the loved boy,
Crowns him with flowers, and makes him all her joy.
And now they never meet in grove or green,
By fountain clear, or spangled starlight sheen,
But they do square, that all their elves for fear   30
Creep into acorn cups and hide them there.

Fairy

Either I mistake your shape and making quite,
Or else you are that shrewd and knavish sprite
Call'd Robin Goodfellow. Are not you he
That frights the maidens of the villagery,   35
Skim milk, and sometimes labor in the quern,
And bootless make the breathless housewife churn,
And sometime make the drink to bear no barm,
Mislead night wanderers, laughing at their harm?
Those that Hobgoblin call you, and sweet Puck,   40
You do their work, and they shall have good luck.
Are not you he?

Puck

                    Thou speak'st aright.
I am that merry wanderer of the night.
I jest to Oberon, and make him smile,   45
When I a fat and bean-fed horse beguile,
Neighing in likeness of a filly foal.
And sometime lurk I in a gossip's bowl,
In very likeness of a roasted crab,
And when she drinks, against her lips I bob   50
And on her withered dewlap pour the ale.
The wisest aunt, telling the saddest tale,
Sometime for three-foot stool mistaketh me.
Then slip I from her bum, down topples she,
And "tailor" cries, and falls into a cough;   55
And then the whole quire hold their hips and laugh,
And waxen in their mirth, and neeze, and swear

58 **wasted**   spent
59 **room**   make room

60 **train**   followers

64 **rash**   hasty
   wanton   spoiled child

67 **Corin**   name of shepherd
68 **corn**   oat stalks
   versing love   making love verses
70 **steppe**   mountain range
71 **bouncing**   big and lusty
   Amazon   refers to Hippolyta
72 **buskin'd**   wearing half-boots
73 **must be**   is to be

76 **Glance**   reflect on my reputation by mentioning Hippolyta

79 **ravished**   kidnapped

81 **Ariadne**   daughter of Minos, King of Crete
   Antiopa   Amazon queen

83 **middle**   beginning of midsummer

A merrier hour was never wasted there.
But, room, fairy! Here comes Oberon.

Fairy

And here my mistress. Would that he were gone!   60

> *Enter, from one side, Oberon, with his train; from
> the other, Titania, with hers.*

Oberon

Ill met by moonlight, proud Titania.

Titania

What, jealous Oberon! Fairies, skip hence.
I have forsworn his bed and company.

Oberon

Tarry, rash wanton. Am not I thy lord?

Titania

Then I must be thy lady. But I know   65
When thou hast stolen away from fairy land,
And in the shape of Corin sat all day,
Playing on pipes of corn, and versing love
To amorous Phillida. Why art thou here,
Come from the farthest steppe of India?   70
But that, forsooth, the bouncing Amazon,
Your buskin'd mistress and your warrior love,
To Theseus must be wedded, and you come
To give their bed joy and prosperity.

Oberon

How canst thou thus for shame, Titania,   75
Glance at my credit with Hippolyta,
Knowing I know thy love to Theseus?
Didst thou not lead him through the glimmering
     night
From Perigenia, whom he ravished?
And make him with fair Aegle break his faith,   80
With Ariadne and Antiopa?

Titania

These are the forgeries of jealousy;
And never, since the middle summer's spring,

85 **rushy**   edged with rushes (marsh plants)
86 **margent**   edge; shore
87 **ringlets**   dances in a small ring

91 **Contagious**   fogs were supposed to spread disease
92 **pelting**   unimportant
93 **overborne**   overflowed their banks

95 **corn**   grain
96 **his**   its

98 **murrion**   dead with a cattle disease
99 **nine men's morris**   a kind of bowling game
100 **quaint mazes**   elaborate, winding paths

102 **want**   lack

105 **washes the air**   the moon is often described as watery

107 **distemperature**   bad weather

110 **Hiems**   god of winter

113 **childing**   fruitful
    change   exchange
115 **increase**   production

118 **original**   source

Met we on hill, in dale, forest, or mead,
By paved fountain or by rushy brook,   85
Or in the beached margent of the sea,
To dance our ringlets to the whistling wind,
But with thy brawls thou hast disturb'd our sport.
Therefore the winds, piping to us in vain,
As in revenge, have suck'd up from the sea   90
Contagious fogs; which, falling in the land,
Have every pelting river made so proud,
That they have overborne their continents.
The ox hath therefore stretch'd his yoke in vain,
The ploughman lost his sweat, and the green corn   95
Hath rotted ere his youth attain'd a beard.
The fold stands empty in the drowned field,
And crows are fatted with the murrion flock;
The nine men's morris is fill'd up with mud;
And the quaint mazes in the wanton green,   100
For lack of tread, are undistinguishable.
The human mortals want their winter here;
No night is now with hymn or carol blest.
Therefore the moon, the governess of floods,
Pale in her anger, washes all the air,   105
That rheumatic diseases do abound.
And thorough this distemperature we see
The seasons alter: hoary-headed frosts
Fall in the fresh lap of the crimson rose,
And on old Hiems' thin and icy crown   110
An odorous chaplet of sweet summer buds
Is, as in mockery, set. The spring, the summer,
The childing autumn, angry winter, change
Their wonted liveries; and the mazed world,
By their increase, now knows not which is which.   115
And this same progeny of evils comes
From our debate, from our dissension;
We are their parents and original.

Oberon

Do you amend it, then; it lies in you.
Why should Titania cross her Oberon?   120

121 **changeling** the boy was the son of an Indian king
122 **henchman** page

125 **votaress** a devoted female

129 **traders** merchant ships

142 **round** dance in a ring

144 **spare** avoid

147 **chide** speak in anger

148 **from** go away from
149 **injury** insult

I do but beg a little changeling boy,
To be my henchman.

Titania

                Set your heart at rest.
The fairy land buys not the child of me.
His mother was a votaress of my order,   125
And, in the spiced Indian air, by night,
Full often hath she gossip'd by my side,
And sat with me on Neptune's yellow sands,
Marking the embarked traders on the flood;
When we have laugh'd to see the sails conceive   130
And grow big-bellied with the wanton wind,
Which she, with pretty and with swimming gait
Following—her womb then rich with my young
    squire—
Would imitate, and sail upon the land,
To fetch me trifles, and return again,   135
As from a voyage, rich with merchandise.
But she, being mortal, of that boy did die,
And for her sake do I rear up her boy,
And for her sake I will not part with him.

Oberon

How long within this wood intend you stay?   140

Titania

Perchance till after Theseus' wedding day.
If you will patiently dance in our round,
And see our moonlight revels, go with us.
If not, shun me, and I will spare your haunts.

Oberon

Give me that boy, and I will go with thee.   145

Titania

Not for thy fairy kingdom. Fairies, away!
We shall chide downright, if I longer stay.
              [*Exit Titania with her Train.*

Oberon

Well, go thy way. Thou shalt not from this grove
Till I torment thee for this injury.

My gentle Puck, come hither. Thou rememberest   150
Since once I sat upon a promontory,
And heard a mermaid, on a dolphin's back,
Uttering such dulcet and harmonious breath,
That the rude sea grew civil at her song,
And certain stars shot madly from their spheres,   155
To hear the sea-maid's music.

Puck

                I remember.

Oberon

That very time I saw, but thou couldst not,
Flying between the cold moon and the earth,
Cupid all arm'd. A certain aim he took   160
At a fair vestal throned by the west,
And loosed his love shaft smartly from his bow,
As it should pierce a hundred thousand hearts.
But I might see young Cupid's fiery shaft
Quench'd in the chaste beams of the watery moon,   165
And the imperial votaress passed on,
In maiden meditation, fancy-free.
Yet mark'd I where the bolt of Cupid fell.
It fell upon a little western flower,
Before milk-white, now purple with love's wound,   170
And maidens call it love-in-idleness.
Fetch me that flower; the herb I shew'd thee once.
The juice of it on sleeping eyelids laid
Will make or man or woman madly dote
Upon the next live creature that it sees.   175
Fetch me this herb, and be thou here again
Ere the leviathan can swim a league.

Puck

I'll put a girdle round about the earth
In forty minutes.

                      [*Exit.*

Oberon

           Having once this juice,   180
I'll watch Titania when she is asleep,
And drop the liquor of it in her eyes.

185 **busy**   mischievous
186 **soul**   highest expression

196 **wode**   insane

199 **draw**   attract
    adamant   magnet; lodestone
201 **leave**   give up

203 **speak you fair**   speak well of you

207 **spaniel**   dog (a servile person)

210 **neglect**   ignore

The next thing then she waking looks upon,
Be it on lion, bear, or wolf, or bull,
On meddling monkey, or on busy ape,   185
She shall pursue it with the soul of love.
And ere I take this charm from off her sight,
As I can take it with another herb,
I'll make her render up her page to me.
But who comes here? I am invisible,   190
And I will overhear their conference.

Enter Demetrius, Helena following him.

Demetrius
I love thee not, therefore pursue me not.
Where is Lysander and fair Hermia?
The one I'll slay, the other slayeth me.
Thou told'st me they were stolen unto this wood,   195
And here am I, and wode within this wood,
Because I cannot meet my Hermia.
Hence, get thee gone, and follow me no more.

Helena
You draw me, you hardhearted adamant,
But yet you draw not iron, for my heart   200
Is true as steel. Leave you your power to draw,
And I shall have no power to follow you.

Demetrius
Do I entice you? Do I speak you fair?
Or, rather, do I not in plainest truth
Tell you, I do not nor I cannot love you?   205

Helena
And even for that do I love you the more.
I am your spaniel and, Demetrius,
The more you beat me, I will fawn on you.
Use me but as your spaniel, spurn me, strike me,
Neglect me, lose me. Only give me leave,   210
Unworthy as I am, to follow you.
What worser place can I beg in your love—
And yet a place of high respect with me—
Than to be used as you use your dog?

218 **impeach** discredit; bring under suspicion

222 **desert** uninhabited

224 **virtue** extreme attractiveness
    privilege protection

231 **brakes** thick undergrowth

234 **story** myth (animal nature and human nature will be
    reversed)
235 **Apollo, etc. . .** in mythology the opposite happens
236 **griffin** beast with an eagle's head and a lion's body

239 **stay thy questions** wait to hear you speak

241 **But** but that

244 **set a scandal on** disgrace

Demetrius
   Tempt not too much the hatred of my spirit,   215
   For I am sick when I do look on thee.

Helena
   And I am sick when I look not on you.

Demetrius
   You do impeach your modesty too much,
   To leave the city, and commit yourself
   Into the hands of one that loves you not;   220
   To trust the opportunity of night
   And the ill counsel of a desert place
   With the rich worth of your virginity.

Helena
   Your virtue is my privilege. For that
   It is not night when I do see your face,   225
   Therefore I think I am not in the night;
   Nor doth this wood lack worlds of company,
   For you in my respect are all the world.
   Then how can it be said I am alone,
   When all the world is here to look on me?   230

Demetrius
   I'll run from thee and hide me in the brakes,
   And leave thee to the mercy of wild beasts.

Helena
   The wildest hath not such a heart as you.
   Run when you will, the story shall be changed.
   Apollo flies, and Daphne holds the chase;   235
   The dove pursues the griffin; the mild hind
   Makes speed to catch the tiger; bootless speed,
   When cowardice pursues, and valor flies.

Demetrius
   I will not stay thy questions. Let me go!
   Or, if thou follow me, do not believe   240
   But I shall do thee mischief in the wood.

Helena
   Aye, in the temple, in the town, the field,
   You do me mischief. Fie, Demetrius!
   Your wrongs do set a scandal on my sex.

248 **To die** by dying
    upon by

254 **blows** blossoms

257 **eglantine** sweet brier

260 **throws** sheds
261 **Weed** garment
262 **streak her eyes** rub her eyelids

271 **fond** doting
272 **ere the first cock crow** before midnight

We cannot fight for love, as men may do; 245
We should be woo'd, and were not made to woo.
> [*Exit Demetrius.*
I'll follow thee, and make a heaven of hell,
To die upon the hand I love so well.
> [*Exit.*

Oberon

Fare thee well, nymph. Ere he do leave this grove
Thou shalt fly him, and he shall seek thy love. 250

> *Reenter Puck.*

Hast thou the flower there? Welcome, wanderer.

Puck

Aye, there it is.

Oberon

I pray thee, give it me.
I know a bank where the wild thyme blows,
Where oxlips and the nodding violet grows, 255
Quite over-canopied with luscious woodbine,
With sweet musk roses, and with eglantine.
There sleeps Titania sometime of the night,
Lull'd in these flowers with dances and delight;
And there the snake throws her enamell'd skin, 260
Weed wide enough to wrap a fairy in.
And with the juice of this I'll streak her eyes,
And make her full of hateful fantasies.
Take thou some of it, and seek through this grove.
A sweet Athenian lady is in love 265
With a disdainful youth. Anoint his eyes,
But do it when the next thing he espies
May be the lady. Thou shalt know the man
By the Athenian garments he hath on.
Effect it with some care that he may prove 270
More fond on her than she upon her love.
And look thou meet me ere the first cock crow.

Puck

Fear not, my lord, your servant shall do so.
> [*Exeunt.*

1 **roundel** dance in a ring

3 **cankers** worms eating rosebuds
4 **reremice** bats

6 **clamorous** wailing
7 **quaint** fine, dainty
8 **offices** duties

9 **double** forked

11 **Newts** poisonous lizards
   blindworms legless lizards

13 **Philomel** nightingale

21 **spinners** spiders

Scene 2. *Another part of the wood*

Enter Titania, with her train.

Titania
Come, now a roundel and a fairy song;
Then, for the third part of a minute, hence—
Some to kill cankers in the musk-rose buds,
Some war with reremice for their leathern wings,
To make my small elves coats, and some keep back   5
The clamorous owl, that nightly hoots and wonders
At our quaint spirits. Sing me now asleep.
Then to you offices, and let me rest.

Song.

First Fairy
You spotted snakes with double tongue,
Thorny hedgehogs, be not seen;   10
Newts and blindworms, do no wrong,
Come not near our fairy queen.

Chorus.

Philomel, with melody,
Sing in our sweet lullaby;
Lulla, lulla, lullaby, lulla, lulla, lullaby: 15
Never harm,
Nor spell, nor charm,
Come our lovely lady nigh.
So, good night, with lullaby.

First Fairy
Weaving spiders, come not here;   20
Hence, you long-legg'd spinners, hence!
Beetles black, approach not near;
Worm nor snail, do no offense.

Chorus.

Philomel, with melody, etc.

Second Fairy
Hence, away! Now all is well: 25

28 **true-love** fiancé

30 **ounce** small leopard
   cat wildcat
31 **Pard** leopard

36 **troth** truthfully

38 **comfort** help

42 **troth** faithful love

45 **take . . . innocence** interpret the meaning as innocent
46 **Love . . . conference** lovers should understand each
   other

One aloof stand sentinel.

[Exeunt Fairies. Titania sleeps.

*Enter Oberon, and squeezes the flower on
Titania's eyelids.*

Oberon

What thou seest when thou dost wake,
Do it for thy true-love take;
Love and languish for his sake.
Be it ounce, or cat, or bear,   30
Pard, or boar with bristled hair,
In thy eye that shall appear
When thou wakest, it is thy dear.
Wake when some vile thing is near.

[Exit.

Enter Lysander and Hermia.

Lysander

Fair love, you faint with wandering in the wood;   35
  And to speak troth, I have forgot our way.
We'll rest us, Hermia, if you think it good
  And tarry for the comfort of the day.

Hermia

Be it so, Lysander. Find you out a bed;
For I upon this bank will rest my head.   40

Lysander

One turf shall serve as pillow for us both,
One heart, one bed, two bosoms, and one troth.

Hermia

Nay, good Lysander. For my sake, my dear,
Lie further off yet, do not lie so near.

Lysander

O, take the sense, sweet, of my innocence!   45
Love takes the meaning in love's conference.
I mean, that my heart unto yours is knit,
So that but one heart we can make of it:
Two bosoms interchained with an oath,

52 **lie** speak falsehoods

53 **prettily** skillfully
54 **beshrew** curse

57 **human** courteous

65 **press'd** pressed down in sleep

68 **approve** test

71 **Weeds** clothes

78 **Churl** rude person
79 **owe** own
80 **When thou wakest . . .** let love make you sleepless

So then two bosoms and a single troth.   50
Then by your side no bed-room me deny;
For lying so, Hermia, I do not lie.

Hermia

Lysander riddles very prettily.
Now much beshrew my manners and my pride,
If Hermia meant to say Lysander lied.   55
But, gentle friend, for love and courtesy
Lie further off. In human modesty,
Such separation as may well be said
Becomes a virtuous bachelor and a maid,
So far be distant: and, good night, sweet friend.   60
Thy love ne'er alter till thy sweet life end!

Lysander

Amen, amen, to that fair prayer, say I,
And then end life when I end loyalty!
Here is my bed. Sleep give thee all his rest!

Hermia

With half that wish the wisher's eyes be press'd!   65

                                  [*They sleep.*

   Enter Puck.

Puck

Through the forest have I gone,
But Athenian found I none,
On whose eyes I might approve
This flower's force in stirring love.
Night and silence. Who is here?   70
Weeds of Athens he doth wear.
This is he, my master said,
Despised the Athenian maid;
And here the maiden, sleeping sound,
On the dank and dirty ground.   75
Pretty soul! She durst not lie
Near this lack-love, this kill-courtesy.
Churl, upon thy eyes I throw
All the power this charm doth owe.
When thou wakest, let love forbid   80

85 **haunt** follow persistently

86 **darkling** in the dark

87 **Stay, on thy peril** you'll be in danger if you don't stay

88 **fond** foolish
89 **lesser in my grace** the less favor I win
90 **lies** dwells
91 **attractive** magnetic

98 **dissembling** deceiving
  glass mirror
99 **sphery eyne** starry eyes

104 **Transparent** very bright (refers to blond beauty)

Sleep his seat on thy eyelid.
So awake when I am gone,
For I must now to Oberon.

[*Exit.*

Enter Demetrius and Helena, running.

Helena
Stay, though thou kill me, sweet Demetrius.
Demetrius
I charge thee, hence, and do not haunt me thus.   85
Helena
O, wilt thou darkling leave me? Do not so.
Demetrius
Stay, on thy peril. I alone will go.

[*Exit.*

Helena
O, I am out of breath in this fond chase!
The more my prayer, the lesser is my grace.
Happy is Hermia, wheresoe'er she lies,   90
For she hath blessed and attractive eyes.
How came her eyes so bright? Not with salt tears.
If so, my eyes are oftener wash'd than hers.
No, no, I am as ugly as a bear,
For beasts that meet me run away for fear.   95
Therefore no marvel though Demetrius
Do, as a monster, fly my presence thus.
What wicked and dissembling glass of mine
Made me compare with Hermia's sphery eyne?
But who is here? Lysander! On the ground!   100
Dead? Or asleep? I see no blood, no wound.
Lysander, if you live, good sir, awake.
Lysander
[*Awaking*] And run through fire I will for thy sweet
     sake.
Transparent Helena! Nature shews art,
That though thy bosom makes me see thy heart.   105

109 **What though**   what difference does it make?

110 **content**   calm

115 **will**   desire

118 **ripe . . . reason**   not mature enough to reason
119 **point**   apex
120 **marshal . . . . will**   force commanding my desires
121 **o'erlook**   look over; survey
122 **Love's stories**   love's true stories

123 **keen**   bitter

127 **Deserve**   win
128 **flout**   jeer at; insult
129 **troth**   upon my word
     good sooth   in very truth

132 **gentleness**   courtesy; refinement

134 **abused**   ill-used

Where is Demetrius? O, how fit a word
Is that vile name to perish on my sword!

Helena

Do not say so, Lysander, say not so.
What though he love your Hermia? Lord, what
    though?
Yet Hermia still loves you. Then be content.   110

Lysander

Content with Hermia! No, I do repent
The tedious minutes I with her have spent.
Not Hermia but Helena I love.
Who will not change a raven for a dove?
The will of man is by his reason sway'd   115
And reason says you are the worthier maid.
Things growing are not ripe until their season.
So, I being young, till now ripe not to reason,
And touching now the point of human skill,
Reason becomes the marshal to my will,   120
And leads me to your eyes, where I o'erlook
Love's stories, written in love's richest book.

Helena

Wherefore was I to this keen mockery born?
When at your hands did I deserve this scorn?
Is't not enough, is't not enough, young man,   125
That I did never, no, nor never can,
Deserve a sweet look from Demetrius' eye,
But you must flout my insufficiency?
Good troth, you do me wrong, good sooth, you do,
In such disdainful manner me to woo.   130
But fare you well. Perforce I must confess
I thought you lord of more true gentleness.
O, that a lady, of one man refused,
Should of another therefore be abused!

                                  [*Exit.*

Lysander

She sees not Hermia. Hermia, sleep thou there.   135
And never mayst thou come Lysander near!

137 **surfeit** excess

140 **of** by
141 **heresy** false belief

143 **address** apply

150 **prey** preying

153 **an if** if
154 **of all loves** if you love me at all

For as a surfeit of the sweetest things
The deepest loathing to the stomach brings,
Or as the heresies that men do leave
Are hated most of those they did deceive,   140
So thou, my surfeit and my heresy,
Of all be hated, but the most of me!
And, all my powers, address your love and might
To honor Helen and to be her knight!

           [*Exit.*

Hermia

[*Awaking*] Help me, Lysander, help me! Do thy best 145
To pluck this crawling serpent from my breast!
Aye me, for pity! What a dream was here!
Lysander, look how I do quake with fear.
Methought a serpent eat my heart away,
And you sat smiling at his cruel prey.   150
Lysander! What, removed? Lysander! Lord!
What, out of hearing? Gone? No sound, no word?
Alack, where are you? Speak, an if you hear;
Speak, of all loves! I swoon almost with fear.
No? Then I well perceive you are not nigh.   155
Either death or you I'll find immediately.

           [*Exit.*

2 pat on the dot

4 tiring house attiring house (actors' dressing room)

7 Bully my fine fellow
Bottom name shows his trade as a weaver. A *bottom* is a ball of thread.

11 abide stand

12 lakin lady kin; by our Lady (the Virgin)
parlous perilous; risky
13 when all is done after all

ACT III

Scene 1. *The wood. Titania lying asleep*

Enter Quince, Snug, Bottom, Flute, Snout, and Starveling.

Bottom
Are we all met?

Quince
Pat, pat; and here's a marvelous convenient place for
our rehearsal. This green plot shall be our stage, this
hawthorn brake our tiring house, and we will do it
in action as we will do it before the duke.   5

Bottom
Peter Quince—

Quince
What sayest thou, Bully Bottom?

Bottom
There are things in this comedy of Pyramus and
Thisby that will never please. First, Pyramus must
draw a sword to kill himself, which the ladies cannot   10
abide. How answer you that?

Snout
By'r lakin, a parlous fear.

Starveling
I believe we must leave the killing out, when all is
done.

Bottom
Not a whit. I have a device to make all well: 15
Write me a prologue, and let the prologue seem to

23 **eight and six** lines of 8 syllables alternating with lines of 6 syllables, a common ballad meter

28 **Masters** gentlemen

30 **fearful** dreadful

37 **defect** Bottom means *effect*. Bottom often blunders with words.
39 **my life for yours** I pledge my life to defend yours
40 **it . . . life** my life would be in danger

say, we will do no harm with our swords, and that
Pyramus is not killed indeed; and, for the more better
assurance, tell them that I Pyramus am not Pyramus,
but Bottom the weaver. This will put them out of   20
fear.

Quince
Well, we will have such a prologue, and it shall be
written in eight and six.

Bottom
No, make it two more. Let it be written in eight and
eight.   25

Snout
Will not the ladies be afeard of the lion?

Starveling
I fear it, I promise you.

Bottom
Masters, you ought to consider with yourselves. To
bring in—God shield us!—a lion among ladies, is a
most dreadful thing; for there is not a more fearful   30
wild fowl than your lion living, and we ought to look
to't.

Snout
Therefore another prologue must tell he is not a lion.

Bottom
Nay, you must name his name, and half his face
must be seen through the lion's neck, and he himself   35
must speak through, saying thus, or to the same
defect—"Ladies,"—or, "Fair ladies—I would wish
you,"—or, "I would request you,"—or, "I would
entreat you—not to fear, not to tremble: my life for
yours. If you think I come hither as a lion, it were   40
pity of my life. No, I am no such thing. I am a man
as other men are." And there indeed let him name
his name, and tell them plainly, he is Snug the joiner.

Quince
Well, it shall be so. But there is two hard things. That

51 great chamber   hall of a great house

53 casement   window frame

54 bush of thorns   English rural folk saw "the man in the
moon" as carrying sticks on his back
55 disfigure   blunder for prefigure
56 present   represent

62 rough-cast   coarse mixture used to plaster outside
walls

is, to bring the moonlight into a chamber, for, you   45
know, Pyramus and Thisby meet by moonlight.

Snout

Doth the moon shine that night we play our play?

Bottom

A calendar, a calendar! Look in the almanac; find out
moonshine, find out moonshine.

Quince

Yes, it doth shine that night.   50

Bottom

Why then may you leave a casement of the great
chamber window, where we play, open, and the
moon may shine in at the casement.

Quince

Aye, or else one must come in with a bush of thorns
and a lantern, and say he comes to disfigure, or to   55
present, the person of moonshine. Then, there is
another thing: we must have a wall in the great
chamber, for Pyramus and Thisby, says the story, did
talk through the chink of a wall.

Snout

You can never bring in a wall. What say you, Bottom?   60

Bottom

Some man or other must present wall. And let him
have some plaster, or some loam, or some rough-cast
about him, to signify wall. And let him hold his
fingers thus, and through that cranny shall Pyramus
and Thisby whisper.   65

Quince

If that may be, then all is well. Come, sit down, every
mother's son, and rehearse your parts. Pyramus, you
begin. When you have spoken your speech, enter
into that brake, and so every one according to his
cue.   70

   Enter Robin (Puck)

71 **hempen home-spuns** rustics lacking grace and polish

73 **toward** in preparation

76 **odious** blunder for odorous

84 **Aye, marry** yes, indeed

88 **triumphant** glorious
89 **brisky juvenal** lively youth
Jew a nonsensical repetition of the first syllable of juvenal

92 **Ninus** mythical founder of Nineveh at whose tomb the lovers would meet

Puck

What hempen homespuns have we swaggering here,
So near the cradle of the fairy queen?
What, a play toward! I'll be an auditor.
An actor too perhaps, if I see cause.

Quince

Speak, Pyramus. Thisby, stand forth.   75

Bottom

Thisby, the flowers of odious savors sweet—

Quince

Odors, odors.

Bottom

—odors savors sweet:
So hath thy breath, my dearest Thisby dear.
But hark, a voice! Stay thou but here awhile,   80
And by and by I will to thee appear.

[*Exit.*

Puck

A stranger Pyramus than e'er play'd here.

[*Exit.*

Flute

Must I speak now?

Quince

Aye, marry must you, for you must understand he
goes but to see a noise that he heard, and is to come   85
again.

Flute

Most radiant Pyramus, most lily-white of hue,
Of color like the red rose on triumphant brier,
Most brisky juvenal, and eke most lovely Jew,
As true as truest horse, that yet would never tire,   90
I'll meet thee, Pyramus, at Ninny's tomb.

Quince

"Ninus' tomb," man. Why, you must not speak that
yet. That you answer to Pyramus. You speak all your
part at once, cues and all. Pyramus enter. Your cue
is past; it is, "never tire."   95

97 **fair** handsome
   were would be

100 **about a round** roundabout

103 **fire** will-o'-the-wisp (deceptive glow)

109 **you see an ass-head of your own** what you think you
    see on me you merely imagine in your own head

111 **translated** transformed

Flute

O—As true as truest horse, that yet would never tire.

Reenter Puck, and Bottom with an ass's head.

Bottom

If I were fair, Thisby, I were only thine.

Quince

O monstrous! O strange! We are haunted. Pray, masters! Fly, masters! Help!

[*Exeunt Quince, Snug, Flute, Snout, and Starveling.*

Puck

I'll follow you, I'll lead you about a round,   100
Through bog, through bush, through brake, through brier.
Sometime a horse I'll be, sometime a hound,
A hog, a headless bear, sometime a fire.
And neigh, and bark, and grunt, and roar, and burn,
Like horse, hound, hog, bear, fire, at every turn.   105

[*Exit.*

Bottom

Why do they run away? This is a knavery of them to make me afeard.

Reenter Snout.

Snout

O Bottom, thou art changed! What do I see on thee?

Bottom

What do you see? You see an ass-head of your own, do you?   110

[*Exit Snout.*

Reenter Quince.

Quince

Bless thee, Bottom! Bless thee! Thou art translated.

[*Exit.*

Bottom

I see their knavery. This is to make an ass of me, to fright me, if they could. But I will not stir from this

117 **ousel** blackbird

119 **throstle** song thrush
120 **quill** piping note

124 **plain-song** simple air (melody with no variation)

127 **who ... etc.** who would apply his mind to answering
    so foolish a bird?
128 **give a bird the lie** call a bird a liar
129 **never so** ever so much

133 **thy fair virtue's force** the power of your beauty

139 **gleek** jest; scoff

place, do what they can. I will walk up and down
here, and I will sing, that they shall hear I am not   115
afraid.

                                                    [*Sings.*

The ousel cock so black of hue,
    With orange-tawny bill,
The throstle with his note so true,
    The wren with little quill;   120

Titania
    [*Awaking*] What angel wakes me from my flowery
    bed?

Bottom
    [*Sings*]   The finch, the sparrow, and the lark,
        The plain-song cuckoo gray,
    Whose note full many a man doth mark,   125
        And dares not answer nay—

    for, indeed, who would set his wit to so foolish a
    bird? Who would give a bird the lie, though he cry
    "cuckoo" never so?

Titania
    I pray thee, gentle mortal, sing again.   130
    Mine ear is much enamor'd of thy note,
    So is mine eye enthralled to thy shape,
    And thy fair virtue's force perforce doth move me
    On the first view to say, to swear, I love thee.

Bottom
    Methinks, mistress, you should have little reason for 135
    that. And yet, to say the truth, reason and love keep
    little company together now-a-days; the more the
    pity, that some honest neighbors will not make them
    friends. Nay, I can gleek upon occasion.

Titania
    Thou art as wise as thou art beautiful.   140

Bottom
    Not so, neither. But if I had wit enough to get out
    of this wood, I have enough to serve mine own turn.

145 **rate** value
146 **summer . . . state** the summer is always present as one of my followers

149 **jewels** precious stones supposedly come from the bottom of the sea

160 **gambol** skip about in play

164 **crop** snip off

166 **have** attend

Titania
 Out of this wood do not desire to go.
 Thou shalt remain here, whether thou wilt or no.
 I am a spirit of no common rate.   145
 The summer still doth tend upon my state;
 And I do love thee. Therefore, go with me.
 I'll give thee fairies to attend on thee,
 And they shall fetch thee jewels from the deep,
 And sing, while thou on pressed flowers dost sleep. 150
 And I will purge thy mortal grossness so,
 That thou shalt like an airy spirit go.
 Peaseblossom! Cobweb! Moth! and Mustardseed!

  Enter Peaseblossom, Cobweb, Moth, and
  Mustardseed.

First Fairy
 Ready.
Second Fairy
   And I.   155
Third Fairy
     And I.
Fourth Fairy
      And I.
All
        Where shall we go?
Titania
 Be kind and courteous to this gentleman.
 Hop in his walks, and gambol in his eyes,   160
 Feed him with apricocks and dewberries,
 With purple grapes, green figs, and mulberries.
 The honey bags steal from the humblebees,
 And for night tapers crop their waxen thighs,
 And light them at the fiery glowworm's eyes, 165
 To have my love to bed and to arise;
 And pluck the wings from painted butterflies,
 To fan the moonbeams from his sleeping eyes.
 Nod to him, elves, and do him courtesies.

First Fairy
　　Hail, mortal!   170
Second Fairy
　　Hail!
Third Fairy
　　Hail!
Fourth Fairy
　　Hail!
Bottom
　　I cry your worship's mercy, heartily. I beseech your
　　worship's name.   175
Cobweb
　　Cobweb.
Bottom
　　I shall desire you of more acquaintance, good Master
　　Cobweb. If I cut my finger, I shall make bold with
　　you. Your name, honest gentleman?
Peaseblossom
　　Peaseblossom.   180
Bottom
　　I pray you, commend me to Mistress Squash, your
　　mother, and to Master Peascod, your father. Good
　　Master Peaseblossom, I shall desire you of more
　　acquaintance too. Your name, I beseech you, sir?
Mustardseed
　　Mustardseed.   185
Bottom
　　Good Master Mustardseed, I know your patience
　　well. That same cowardly, giantlike ox-beef hath
　　devoured many a gentleman of your house. I promise
　　you your kindred hath made my eyes water ere now.
　　I desire your more acquaintance, good Master   190
　　Mustardseed.
Titania
　　Come, wait upon him; lead him to my bower.
　　The moon methinks looks with a watery eye,

194 **when she weeps** when she causes dew to form
195 **enforced** violated

2 **next** nearest (the first)
3 **in extremity** extremely

6 **night-rule** mischief; night sport
   haunted frequented

8 **close** secret
9 **dull** drowsy
10 **patches** fools; clowns
   rude mechanicals ignorant merchants (laborers)
11 **stalls** shops; market booths

14 **shallowest** most foolish
   thick-skin blockhead
   barren sort stupid bunch

18 **nole** head

20 **mimic** buffoon; actor

22 **russet-pated** gray-headed
   in sort in a flock

And when she weeps, weeps every little flower,
Lamenting some enforced chastity.   195
Tie up my love's tongue, bring him silently.

                              [*Exeunt.*

Scene 2. *Another part of the wood*

Enter Oberon.

Oberon
   I wonder if Titania be awaked.
   Then, what it was that next came in her eye,
   Which she must dote on in extremity.

      Enter Puck.

   Here comes my messenger.
                              How now, mad spirit!   5
   What night-rule now about this haunted grove?
Puck
   My mistress with a monster is in love.
   Near to her close and consecrated bower,
   While she was in her dull and sleeping hour,
   A crew of patches, rude mechanicals,   10
   That work for bread upon Athenian stalls,
   Were met together to rehearse a play,
   Intended for great Theseus' nuptial day.
   The shallowest thickskin of that barren sort,
   Who Pyramus presented, in their sport   15
   Forsook his scene, and enter'd in a brake.
   When I did him at this advantage take,
   An ass's nole I fixed on his head.
   Anon his Thisby must be answered,
   And forth my mimic comes. When they him spy,   20
   As wild geese that the creeping fowler eye,
   Or russet-pated choughs, many in sort,

28 Their ... wrong their weak brains, weakened further by their fears, made inanimate things hurt them

31 from yielders everybody is ready to take advantage of those who give up

33 translated transformed

37 latch'd anointed

41 That so that

42 Stand close hide

44 rebuke criticize sharply
45 breath speech

49 deep the depths of guilt

Rising and cawing at the gun's report,
Sever themselves and madly sweep the sky,
So, at his sight, away his fellows fly.   25
And, at our stamp, here o'er and o'er one falls;
He murder cries, and help from Athens calls.
Their sense thus weak, lost with their fears thus
          strong,
Made senseless things begin to do them wrong.
For briers and thorns at their apparel snatch,   30
Some sleeves, some hats, from yielders all things
          catch.
I led them on in this distracted fear,
And left sweet Pyramus translated there.
When in that moment, so it came to pass,
Titania waked, and straightway loved an ass.   35

Oberon
This falls out better than I could devise.
But hast thou yet latch'd the Athenian's eyes
With a love juice, as I did bid thee do?

Puck
I took him sleeping—that is finish'd too—
And the Athenian woman by his side,   40
That, when he waked, of force she must be eyed.

          Enter Hermia and Demetrius.

Oberon
Stand close. This is the same Athenian.

Puck
This is the woman, but not this the man.

Demetrius
O, why rebuke you him that loves you so?
Lay breath so bitter on your bitter foe.   45

Hermia
Now I but chide; but I should use thee worse,
For thou, I fear, hast given me cause to curse.
If thou hast slain Lysander in his sleep,
Being o'er shoes in blood, plunge in the deep,

54 **whole** solid
   be bored have a hole bored through it
55 **center** center of the earth
56 **brother** sun
   Antipodes other side of the earth
58 **dead** deathly pale

61 **clear** shining

63 **What's this** what has this to do with my Lysander

66 **Out** away with you

71 **brave touch** splendid deed
72 **worm** snake; serpent

75 **misprised mood** mistaken fit of anger

And kill me too.   50
The sun was not so true unto the day
As he to me. Would he have stolen away
From sleeping Hermia? I'll believe as soon
This whole earth may be bored, and that the moon
May through the center creep, and so displease   55
Her brother's noontide with the Antipodes.
It cannot be but thou hast murder'd him.
So should a murderer look, so dead, so grim.

Demetrius

So should the murder'd look, and so should I,
Pierced through the heart with your stern cruelty.   60
Yet you, the murderer, look as bright, as clear,
As yonder Venus in her glimmering sphere.

Hermia

What's this to my Lysander? Where is he?
Ah, good Demetrius, wilt thou give him me?

Demetrius

I had rather give his carcass to my hounds.   65

Hermia

Out, dog! Out, cur! Thou drivest me past the bounds
Of maiden's patience. Hast thou slain him, then?
Henceforth be never number'd among men!
O, once tell true, tell true, even for my sake!
Durst thou have look'd upon him being awake,   70
And hast thou kill'd him sleeping? O brave touch!
Could not a worm, an adder, do so much?
An adder did it; for with doubler tongue
Than thine, thou serpent, never adder stung.

Demetrius

You spend your passion on a misprised mood.   75
I am not guilty of Lysander's blood,
Nor is he dead, for aught that I can tell.

Hermia

I pray thee, tell me then that he is well.

Demetrius

An if I could, what should I get therefore?

83 vein mood

85 So ... pay sleep owes me a chance to rest; but when a man is sad, sleep is like a bankrupt person who cannot pay

88 If ... stay if I wait here a while for sleep to make me an offer

90 true-love's sight on the eyes of a betrothed man

93 Then fate ... fail fate prevents faithfulness. For one faithful man, a million are faithless.

94 confounding oath on oath destroying one oath with another

97 fancy-sick lovesick
   cheer face

98 sighs an ancient belief was that each sigh costs a drop of blood

100 against before

Hermia

    A privilege, never to see me more.   80
    And from thy hated presence part I so.
    See me no more, whether he be dead or no.

                               [*Exit.*

Demetrius

    There is no following her in this fierce vein.
    Here therefore for a while I will remain.
    So sorrow's heaviness doth heavier grow   85
    For debt that bankrupt sleep doth sorrow owe;
    Which now in some slight measure it will pay,
    If for his tender here I make some stay.

                   [*Lies down and sleeps.*

Oberon

    What hast thou done? Thou hast mistaken quite,
    And laid the love juice on some true-love's sight.   90
    Of thy misprision must perforce ensue
    Some true love turn'd, and not a false turn'd true.

Puck

    Then fate o'errules, that, one man holding troth,
    A million fail, confounding oath on oath.

Oberon

    About the wood go swifter than the wind,   95
    And Helena of Athens look thou find.
    All fancy-sick she is and pale of cheer,
    With sighs of love, that costs the fresh blood dear.
    By some illusion see thou bring her here.
    I'll charm his eyes against she do appear.   100

Puck

    I go, I go. Look how I go,
    Swifter than arrow from the Tartar's bow.

                              [*Exit.*

Oberon

    Flower of this purple dye,
    Hit with Cupid's archery,
    Sink in apple of his eye.   105
    When his love he doth espy,

114 **fee**   privilege
115 **fond pageant**   foolish show

120 **sport alone**   for sport and no other reason

122 **preposterously**   contrary to reason

125 **vows so born**   vows, thus born, appear to be pure
truth
126 **nativity**   birth
128 **badge**   family crest

129 **advance**   show

131 **give her o'er**   give her up

134 **even weigh**   have the same weight
tales   lies

Let her shine as gloriously
As the Venus of the sky.
When thou wakest, if she be by,
Beg of her for remedy.   110

Reenter Puck.

Puck
Captain of our fairy band,
Helena is here at hand,
And the youth, mistook by me,
Pleading for a lover's fee.
Shall we their fond pageant see?   115
Lord, what fools these mortals be!

Oberon
Stand aside. The noise they make
Will cause Demetrius to awake.

Puck
Then will two at once woo one;
That must needs be sport alone.   120
And those things do best please me
That befall preposterously.

Enter Lysander and Helena.

Lysander
Why should you think that I should woo in scorn?
Scorn and derision never come in tears.
Look, when I vow, I weep. And vows so born,   125
In their nativity all truth appears.
How can these things in me seem scorn to you,
Bearing the badge of faith, to prove them true?

Helena
You do advance your cunning more and more.
When truth kills truth, O devilish-holy fray!   130
These vows are Hermia's. Will you give her o'er?
Weigh oath with oath, and you will nothing weigh.
Your vows to her and me, put in two scales,
Will even weigh; and both as light as tales.

142 **Taurus**   a mountain range in Asiatic Turkey
143 **turns to a crow**   seems black by comparison

145 **seal**   pledge

147 **set against**   attack

152 **show**   appearance
153 **gentle**   well-born
154 **my parts**   my qualities of mind and body

158 **trim**   fine (used sarcastically)

161 **extort**   torture

Lysander
    I had no judgment when to her I swore.   135
Helena
    Nor none, in my mind, now you give her o'er.
Lysander
    Demetrius loves her, and he loves not you.
Demetrius
    [*Awaking*] O Helen, goddess, nymph, perfect, divine!
    To what, my love, shall I compare thine eyne?
    Crystal is muddy. O, how ripe in show   140
    Thy lips, those kissing cherries, tempting grow!
    That pure congealed white, high Taurus' snow,
    Fann'd with the eastern wind, turns to a crow
    When thou hold'st up thy hand. O, let me kiss
    This princess of pure white, this seal of bliss!   145
Helena
    O spite! O hell! I see you all are bent
    To set against me for your merriment.
    If you were civil and knew courtesy,
    You would not do me thus much injury.
    Can you not hate me, as I know you do,   150
    But you must join in souls to mock me too?
    If you were men, as men you are in show,
    You would not use a gentle lady so;
    To vow, and swear, and superpraise my parts,
    When I am sure you hate me with your hearts.   155
    You both are rivals, and love Hermia,
    And now both rivals, to mock Helena.
    A trim exploit, a manly enterprise,
    To conjure tears up in a poor maid's eyes
    With your derision! None of noble sort   160
    Would so offend a virgin, and extort
    A poor soul's patience, all to make you sport.
Lysander
    You are unkind, Demetrius. Be.not so;
    For you love Hermia; this you know I know.

169 **idle**   useless

170 **I will none**   I have no wish for her

172 **as guestwise sojourn'd**   has made a short stay

177 **aby it dear**   pay dearly for it

179 **his**   its

184 **to thy sound**   to the sound of your voice

188 **bide**   wait

190 **oes**   circles; stars

And here, with all good will, with all my heart,   165
In Hermia's love I yield you up my part;
And yours of Helena to me bequeath,
Whom I do love, and will do till my death.

Helena
Never did mockers waste more idle breath.

Demetrius
Lysander, keep thy Hermia, I will none.   170
If e'er I loved her, all that love is gone.
My heart to her but as guestwise sojourn'd,
And now to Helen is it home return'd,
There to remain.

Lysander
      Helen, it is not so.   175

Demetrius
Disparage not the faith thou dost not know,
Lest, to thy peril, thou aby it dear.
Look, where thy love comes. Yonder is thy dear.

 Reenter Hermia.

Hermia
Dark night, that from the eye his function takes,
The ear more quick of apprehension makes.   180
Wherein it doth impair the seeing sense,
It pays the hearing double recompense.
Thou are not by mine eye, Lysander, found;
Mine ear, I thank it, brought me to thy sound.
But why unkindly didst thou leave me so?   185

Lysander
Why should he stay, whom love doth press to go?

Hermia
What love could press Lysander from my side?

Lysander
Lysander's love, that would not let him bide,
Fair Helena, who more engilds the night
Than all yon fiery oes and eyes of light.   190

196 **in spite of me**   to spite me

198 **contrived**   plotted

200 **counsel**   secrets

202 **chid**   scolded; disapproved of

205 **artificial**   skillful in art

207 **sampler**   a piece of embroidery

210 **incorporate**   parts of the same body
211 **seeming**   apparently
212 **partition**   division
213 **lovely**   loving

216 **Due but to one**   belonging to just one single heart
217 **rent**   tear

222 **amazed**   completely confused

Why seek'st thou me? Could not this make thee
    know,
The hate I bare thee made me leave thee so?

Hermia

You speak not as you think. It cannot be.

Helena

Lo, she is one of this confederacy!
Now I perceive they have conjoin'd all three   195
To fashion this false sport, in spite of me.
Injurious Hermia! Most ungrateful maid!
Have you conspired, have you with these contrived
To bait me with this foul derision?
Is all the counsel that we two have shared,   200
The sisters' vows, the hours that we have spent,
When we have chid the hasty-footed time
For parting us—O, is all forgot?
All school days' friendship, childhood innocence?
We, Hermia, like two artificial gods,   205
Have with our needles created both one flower,
Both on one sampler, sitting on one cushion,
Both warbling of one song, both in one key;
As if our hands, our sides, voices, and minds,
Had been incorporate. So we grew together,   210
Like to a double cherry, seeming parted,
But yet an union in partition;
Two lovely berries moulded on one stem,
So, with two seeming bodies, but one heart;
Two of the first, like coats in heraldry,   215
Due but to one, and crowned with one crest.
And will you rent our ancient love asunder,
To join with men in scorning your poor friend?
It is not friendly, 'tis not maidenly.
Our sex, as well as I, may chide you for it,   220
Though I alone do feel the injury.

Hermia

I am amazed at your passionate words.
I scorn you not. It seems that you scorn me.

Helena

 Have you not set Lysander, as in scorn,
 To follow me and praise my eyes and face?   225
 And made your other love, Demetrius,
 Who even but now did spurn me with his foot,
 To call me goddess, nymph, divine and rare,
 Precious, celestial? Wherefore speaks he this
 To her he hates? And wherefore doth Lysander 230
 Deny your love, so rich within his soul,
 And tender me, forsooth, affection,
 But by your setting on, by your consent?
 What though I be not so in grace as you,
 So hung upon with love, so fortunate,   235
 But miserable most, to love unloved?
 This you should pity rather than despise.

Hermia

 I understand not what you mean by this.

Helena

 Aye, do, persever, counterfeit sad looks,
 Make mouths upon me when I turn my back. 240
 Wink each at other; hold the sweet jest up.
 This sport, well carried, shall be chronicled.
 If you have any pity, grace, or manners,
 You would not make me such an argument.
 But fare ye well. 'Tis partly my own fault,   245
 Which death or absence soon shall remedy.

Lysander

 Stay, gentle Helena, hear my excuse.
 My love, my life, my soul, fair Helena!

Helena

 O excellent!

Hermia

      Sweet, do not scorn her so.   250

Demetrius

 If she cannot entreat, I can compel.

Lysander

 Thou canst compel no more than she entreat.

258 **prove**   prove by a duel

262 **Ethiope**   black one

263 **take on**   make a fuss as if you really wished to follow me

265 **Hang off**   let go

272 **sooth**   truly

273 **I will**   I'll keep my challenge to fight you

274 **bond**   written agreement

Thy threats have no more strength than her weak
    prayers.
Helen, I love thee, by my life, I do.
I swear by that which I will lose for thee,   255
To prove him false that says I love thee not.

Demetrius
I say I love thee more than he can do.

Lysander
If thou say so, withdraw, and prove it too.

Demetrius
Quick, come!

Hermia
                Lysander, whereto tends all this?   260

Lysander
Away, you Ethiope!

Demetrius
                  No, no; you'll
Seem to break loose, take on as you would follow,
But yet come not. You are a tame man, go!

Lysander
Hang off, thou cat, thou burr! Vile thing, let loose,   265
Or I will shake thee from me like a serpent!

Hermia
Why are you grown so rude? What change is this?
Sweet love—

Lysander
             Thy love! Out, tawny Tartar, out!
Out, loathed medicine! Hated potion, hence!   270

Hermia
Do you not jest?

Helena
              Yes, sooth, and so do you.

Lysander
Demetrius, I will keep my word with thee.

Demetrius
I would I had your bond, for I perceive

275 **A weak bond** Hermia's weak grasp

279 **What news** what does this mean?

281 **erewhile** a little while ago
282 **Since night** not so long ago as the beginning of this
night

290 **juggler** deceiver
canker blossom wild rose (as contrasted to the culti-
vated rose)

297 **puppet** doll-like person (suggests smallness)

298 **Why so?** very well

301 **personage** figure

A weak bond holds you. I'll not trust your word.   275

Lysander

What, should I hurt her, strike her, kill her dead?
Although I hate her, I'll not harm her so.

Hermia

What, can you do me greater harm than hate?
Hate me! Wherefore? O me! What news, my love!
Am not I Hermia? Are not you Lysander?   280
I am as fair now as I was erewhile.
Since night you loved me, yet since night you left
          me.
Why, then you left me—O, the gods forbid!—
In earnest, shall I say?

Lysander

                              Aye, by my life!   285
And never did desire to see thee more.
Therefore be out of hope, of question, of doubt;
Be certain, nothing truer. 'Tis no jest
That I do hate thee, and love Helena.

Hermia

O me! You juggler! You canker blossom!   290
You thief of love! What, have you come by night
And stolen my love's heart from him?

Helena

                                        Fine, i' faith!
Have you no modesty, no maiden shame,
No touch of bashfulness? What, will you tear   295
Impatient answers from my gentle tongue?
Fie, fie! You counterfeit, you puppet, you!

Hermia

Puppet? Why so? Aye, that way goes the game.
Now I perceive that she hath made compare
Between our statures; she hath urged her height,   300
And with her personage, her tall personage,
Her height, forsooth, she hath prevail'd with him.
And are you grown so high in his esteem,

304 **low**   short

309 **curst**   ill-tempered
310 **shrewishness**   showing a bad temper
311 **I . . . cowardice**   lacking courage

313 **something**   somewhat
314 **match her**   prove her match in a fight

318 **counsels**   secrets

320 **stealth**   stealing away

323 **spurn**   kick
324 **so**   provided that
325 **my folly**   the burden of my foolish love

327 **fond**   foolish

Because I am so dwarfish and so low?
How low am I, thou painted maypole? Speak.   305
How low am I? I am not yet so low
But that my nails can reach unto thine eyes.

Helena

I pray you, though you mock me, gentlemen,
Let her not hurt me. I was never curst.
I have no gift at all in shrewishness;   310
I am a right maid for my cowardice.
Let her not strike me. You perhaps may think,
Because she is something lower than myself,
That I can match her.

Hermia

                    Lower! hark, again.   315

Helena

Good Hermia, do not be so bitter with me,
I evermore did love you, Hermia,
Did ever keep your counsels, never wrong'd you,
Save that, in love unto Demetrius,
I told him of your stealth unto this wood.   320
He follow'd you; for love I follow'd him.
But he hath chid me hence, and threaten'd me
To strike me, spurn me, nay, to kill me too.
And now, so you will let me quiet go,
To Athens will I bear my folly back,   325
And follow you no further. Let me go.
You see how simple and how fond I am.

Hermia

Why, get you gone. Who is't that hinders you?

Helena

A foolish heart, that I leave here behind.

Hermia

What, with Lysander?   330

Helena

                    With Demetrius.

Lysander

Be not afraid. She shall not harm thee, Helena.

334 **keen and shrewd** sharp of tongue and savage
335 **vixen** female fox; bad-tempered woman

341 **minimus** tiny creature
   knot-grass a growth-stunting weed

343 **officious** volunteering services that are not necessary

346 **intend** pretend

348 **aby** pay dearly for

352 **cheek by jowl** side by side

353 **coil** turmoil
   'long of you on account of you

Demetrius
No, sir, she shall not, though you take her part.

Helena
O, when she's angry, she is keen and shrewd!
She was a vixen when she went to school,   335
And though she be but little, she is fierce.

Hermia
Little again! Nothing but low and little!
Why will you suffer her to flout me thus?
Let me come to her.

Lysander
                  Get you gone, you dwarf.   340
You minimus, of hindering knot-grass made.
You bead, you acorn!

Demetrius
                You are too officious
In her behalf that scorns your services.
Let her alone. Speak not of Helena;   345
Take not her part, for, if thou dost intend
Never so little show of love to her,
Thou shalt aby it.

Lysander
             Now she holds me not.
Now follow, if thou darest, to try whose right,   350
Of thine or mine, is most in Helena.

Demetrius
Follow! Nay, I'll go with thee, cheek by jowl.
          [Exeunt Lysander and Demetrius.

Hermia
You, mistress, all this coil is 'long of you.
Nay, go not back.

Helena
           I will not trust you, I   355
No longer stay in your curst company.
Your hands than mine are quicker for a fray.
My legs are longer though, to run away.
                      [Exit.

359 **amazed** in complete confusion

360 **negligence** carelessness
    Still always

367 **sort** come to pass
368 **jangling** noisy quarreling

370 **Hie** hasten
371 **welkin** sky
372 **Acheron** hell (a river in Hades)

374 **As** so that

376 **wrong** insulting language

380 **batty** batlike
381 **herb** antidote to love-in-idleness
382 **virtuous** powerful

385 **derision** this ridiculous delusion

388 **date** duration

Hermia
  I am amazed, and know not what to say.

                                  [*Exit.*

Oberon
  This is thy negligence. Still thou mistakest, 360
  Or else committ'st thy knaveries willfully.

Puck
  Believe me, king of shadows, I mistook.
  Did not you tell me I should know the man
  By the Athenian garments he had on?
  And so far blameless proves my enterprise, 365
  That I have 'nointed an Athenian's eyes;
  And so far am I glad it so did sort,
  As this their jangling I esteem a sport.

Oberon
  Thou see'st these lovers seek a place to fight.
  Hie therefore, Robin, overcast the night. 370
  The starry welkin cover thou anon
  With drooping fog, as black as Acheron,
  And lead these testy rivals so astray,
  As one come not within another's way.
  Like to Lysander sometime frame thy tongue, 375
  Then stir Demetrius up with bitter wrong;
  And sometime rail thou like Demetrius.
  And from each other look thou lead them thus,
  Till o'er their brows death-counterfeiting sleep
  With leaden legs and batty wings doth creep. 380
  Then crush this herb into Lysander's eye,
  Whose liquor hath this virtuous property,
  To take from thence all error with his might,
  And make his eyeballs roll with wonted sight.
  When they next wake, all this derision 385
  Shall seem a dream and fruitless vision,
  And back to Athens shall the lovers wend,
  With league whose date till death shall never end.
  Whiles I in this affair do thee employ,
  I'll to my queen and beg her Indian boy; 390

394 **night's swift dragons** Shakespeare saw the dragons as yoked to night's chariot

395 **Aurora's harbinger** the approach of dawn

398 **crossways** suicides were buried at crossroads
floods refers to people who have drowned themselves, and whose bodies have not been found

403 **of another sort** not infernal (of the lower world) and thus able to withstand daylight

405 **like** in the guise of

406 **eastern . . . red** the sun rising in the east

407 **Opening on Neptune** shining on the oceans

414 **Goblin** hobgoblin (mischievious spirit); Puck

417 **drawn** with my sword drawn

And then I will her charmed eye release
From monster's view, and all things shall be peace.

Puck

My fairy lord, this must be done with haste,
For night's swift dragons cut the clouds full fast,
And yonder shines Aurora's harbinger,   395
At whose approach, ghosts, wandering here and
      there,
Troop home to churchyards: damned spirits all,
That in crossways and floods have burial,
Already to their wormy beds are gone.
For fear lest day should look their shames upon,   400
They willfully themselves exile from light,
And must for aye consort with black-brow'd night.

Oberon

But we are spirits of another sort.
I with the morning's love have oft made sport,
And, like a forester, the groves may tread   405
Even till the eastern gate, all fiery-red,
Opening on Neptune with fair blessed beams,
Turns into yellow gold his salt green streams.
But, notwithstanding, haste. Make no delay:
We may effect this business yet ere day.   410
                                              [*Exit.*

Puck

            Up and down, up and down,
            I will lead them up and down:
            I am fear'd in field and town.
            Goblin, lead them up and down.
Here comes one.   415

      Reenter Lysander.

Lysander

Where art thou, proud Demetrius? Speak thou now.

Puck

Here, villain, drawn and ready. Where art thou?

418 **straight**   at once

420 **plainer**   more level

426 **recreant**   coward

427 **defiled**   disgraced

430 **try**   test
    manhood   courage

431 **still dares me on**   always challenged me to follow

435 **That**   so that

Lysander
  I will be with thee straight.
Puck
                          Follow me, then,
  To plainer ground.   420
                  [*Exit Lysander, as following the voice.*

     Reenter Demetrius.

Demetrius
  Lysander! Speak again!
  Thou runaway, thou coward, art thou fled?
  Speak! In some bush? Where dost thou hide thy
      head?
Puck
  Thou coward, art thou bragging to the stars,
  Telling the bushes that thou look'st for wars,   425
  And wilt not come? Come, recreant! Come, thou
      child!
  I'll whip thee with a rod. He is defiled
  That draws a sword on thee.
Demetrius
                          Yea, art thou there?
Puck
  Follow my voice. We'll try no manhood here.   430
                                          [*Exeunt.*

     Reenter Lysander.

Lysander
  He goes before me and still dares me on.
  When I come where he calls, then he is gone.
  The villain is much lighter-heel'd than I.
  I follow'd fast, but faster he did fly,
  That fallen am I in dark uneven way,   435
  And here will rest me. [*Lies down.*] Come, thou gentle
      day!
  For if but once thou show me thy gray light,
  I'll find Demetrius, and revenge this spite.
                                          [*Sleeps.*

440 **Abide** wait for
   wot know

445 **buy this dear** pay dearly for this

448 **measure . . . length** stretch out
449 **visited** encountered

451 **Abate** shorten; put an end to
   Shine comforts let comforting light shine

458 **curst** angry; cross

Reenter Puck and Demetrius.

Puck
Ho, ho, ho! Coward, why comest thou not?

Demetrius
Abide me, if thou darest; for well I wot   440
Thou runn'st before me, shifting every place,
And darest not stand, nor look me in the face.
Where art thou now?

Puck
                                    Come hither. I am here.

Demetrius
Nay, then, thou mock'st me. Thou shalt buy this dear,   445
If ever I thy face by daylight see.
Now, go thy way. Faintness constraineth me
To measure out my length on this cold bed.
By day's approach look to be visited.
                              [*Lies down and sleeps.*

Reenter Helena.

Helena
O weary night, O long and tedious night,   450
Abate thy hours! Shine comforts from the east,
That I may back to Athens by daylight,
From these that my poor company detest.
And sleep, that sometimes shuts up sorrow's eye,
Steal me awhile from mine own company.   455
                              [*Lies down and sleeps.*

Puck
                    Yet but three? Come one more.
                    Two of both kinds makes up four.
                    Here she comes, curst and sad.
                    Cupid is a knavish lad,
                    Thus to make poor females mad.   460

Reenter Hermia.

466 they Lysander and Demetrius

482 The man . . . . well everything will be worked out peacefully

Hermia

    Never so weary, never so in woe;
    Bedabbled with the dew, and torn with briers,
    I can no further crawl, no further go.
    My legs can keep no pace with my desires.
    Here will I rest me till the break of day.   465
    Heavens shield Lysander, if they mean a fray!
                      [*Lies down and sleeps.*

Puck

           On the ground
           Sleep sound.
           I'll apply
           To your eye,   470
    Gentle lover, remedy.
           [*Squeezing the juice on Lysander's eye.*
           When thou wakest,
           Thou takest
           True delight
           In the sight   475
    Of thy former lady's eye.
    And the country proverb known,
    That every man should take his own,
    In your waking shall be shown.
           Jack shall have Jill;   480
           Nought shall go ill;
    The man shall have his mare again, and all shall be
      well.
                          [*Exit.*

The four lovers remain asleep on the stage until they are awakened by shouts and horns after Act IV, Scene 1, line 147.

2 **amiable** lovely
coy stroke

16 **overflown with** submerged by

ACT IV

Scene 1. The same. Lysander, Demetrius, Helena, and Hermia, lying asleep

Enter Titania and Bottom; Peaseblossom, Cobweb, Moth, Mustardseed, and other Fairies attending; Oberon behind unseen.

Titania
Come, sit thee down upon this flowery bed,
While I thy amiable cheeks do coy,
And stick musk roses in thy sleek smooth head,
And kiss thy fair large ears, my gentle joy.

Bottom
Where's Peaseblossom?   5

Peaseblossom
Ready.

Bottom
Scratch my head, Peaseblossom. Where's Mounsieur Cobweb?

Cobweb
Ready.

Bottom
Mounsieur Cobweb, good mounsieur, get you your   10
weapons in your hand, and kill me a red-hipped
humble-bee on the top of a thistle; and, good
mounsieur, bring me the honey bag. Do not fret
yourself too much in the action, mounsieur; and,
good mounsieur, have a care the honey bag break   15
not. I would be loth to have you overflown with a
honey bag, signior. Where's Mounsieur Mustardseed.

113

19 **neaf**   hand; fist
20 **leave your courtesy**   stop bowing and scraping (or, put on your hat)

22 **Cavalery**   caballero (Spanish); gentleman

29 **tongs**   a kind of triangle
bones   clappers (he made music by striking metal against a pair of tongs)

32 **bottle**   bundle (of hay)
33 **hath no fellow**   has no equal

37 **stir**   disturb
38 **exposition of**   disposition for (word blunder)

40 **all ways away**   in every direction

Mustardseed
Ready.

Bottom
Give me your neaf, Mounsieur Mustardseed. Pray
you leave your courtesy, good mounsieur.   20

Mustardseed
What's your will?

Bottom
Nothing, good mounsieur, but to help Cavalery
Cobweb to scratch. I must to the barber's,
mounsieur, for methinks I am marvelous hairy about
the face. And I am such a tender ass, if my hair do   25
but tickle me, I must scratch.

Titania
What, wilt thou hear some music, my sweet love?

Bottom
I have a reasonable good ear in music. Let's have
the tongs and the bones.

Titania
Or say, sweet love, what thou desirest to eat.   30

Bottom
Truly, a peck of provender. I could munch your good
dry oats. Methinks I have a great desire to a bottle
of hay. Good hay, sweet hay, hath no fellow.

Titania
I have a venturous fairy that shall seek
The squirrel's hoard, and fetch thee new nuts.   35

Bottom
I had rather have a handful or two of dried peas.
But, I pray you, let none of your people stir me. I
have an exposition of sleep come upon me.

Titania
Sleep thou, and I will wind thee in my arms.
Fairies, be gone, and be all ways away.   40
                              [*Exeunt Fairies.*
So doth the woodbine the sweet honeysuckle

46 **dotage** foolish affection

48 **sweet favors** flowers as love tokens
49 **upbraid** scold; find fault with
50 **rounded** encircled

52 **sometime** formerly
53 **orient pearls** the most beautiful of pearls

60 **bower** shaded retreat; abode

62 **hateful imperfection** seeing Bottom's disguise as de-
sirable
63 **scalp** skull
65 **other** others
66 **May** they may
67 **accidents** happenings
68 **fierce** violent

72 **Dian's bud** a plant to preserve chastity

Gently entwist; the female ivy so.
Enrings the barky fingers of the elm.
O, how I love thee! How I dote on thee!

[*They sleep.*

Enter Puck.

Oberon
[*Advancing*] Welcome, good Robin. See'st thou this   45
    sweet sight?
Her dotage now I do begin to pity;
For, meeting her of late behind the wood,
Seeking sweet favors for this hateful fool,
I did upbraid her, and fall out with her.
For she his hairy temples then had rounded   50
With coronet of fresh and fragrant flowers.
And that same dew, which sometime on the buds
Was wont to swell, like round and orient pearls,
Stood now within the pretty flowerets' eyes,
Like tears, that did their own disgrace bewail.   55
When I had at my pleasure taunted her,
And she in mild terms begg'd my patience,
I then did ask of her her changeling child;
Which straight she gave me, and her fairy sent
To bear him to my bower in fairy land.   60
And now I have the boy, I will undo
This hateful imperfection of her eyes.
And, gentle Puck, take this transformed scalp
From off the head of this Athenian swain;
That, he awaking when the other do,   65
May all to Athens back again repair,
And think no more of this night's accidents,
But as the fierce vexation of a dream.
But first I will release the fairy queen.
    Be as thou wast wont to be;   70
    See as thou wast wont to see.
    Dian's bud o'er Cupid's flower
    Hath such force and blessed power.
Now, my Titania! Wake you, my sweet queen.

81 **strike . . . sleep** make them sleep more soundly than
   normal
82 **these five** Bottom and the four lovers
83 **Music, still** continuous music

88 **solemnly** ceremoniously
89 **triumphantly** festively

95 **sad** serious

Titania
>   My Oberon! What visions have I seen!   75
>   Methought I was enamor'd of an ass.

Oberon
>   There lies your love.

Titania
>   How came these things to pass?
>   O, how mine eyes do loathe his visage now!

Oberon
>   Silence awhile. Robin, take off this head.   80
>   Titania, music call; and strike more dead
>   Than common sleep of all these five the sense.

Titania
>   Music, ho! Music! Such as charmeth sleep!
>   [*Music, still.*

Puck
>   Now, when thou wakest, with thine own fool's eyes
>   peep.

Oberon
>   Sound, music! Come, my queen take hands with me,   85
>   And rock the ground whereon these sleepers be.
>   Now thou and I are new in amity,
>   And will tomorrow midnight solemnly
>   Dance in Duke Theseus' house triumphantly,
>   And bless it to all fair prosperity.   90
>   There shall the pairs of faithful lovers be
>   Wedded, with Theseus, all in jollity.

Puck
>   Fairy king, attend, and mark.
>   I do hear the morning lark.

Oberon
>   Then, my queen, in silence sad,   95
>   Trip we after night's shade.
>   We the globe can compass soon,
>   Swifter than the wandering moon.

104 **observation** May Day rites
105 **vaward** earliest part

107 **Uncouple** unleash
108 **Dispatch** hurry

113 **bay'd the bear** cut off the bear's retreat
114 **hounds of Sparta** famous for hunting ability
115 **chiding** baying

120 **flew'd** suggests loose parts of upper lip of a hound
    sanded having the color of sand
122 **Crook-knee'd** curving
    dew-lapp'd having a pendulous flap of skin at the
    throat
123 **match'd . . . bells** with voices of varying pitch

Titania

    Come, my lord, and in our flight,
    Tell me how it came this night,   100
    That I sleeping here was found
    With these mortals on the ground.

                      [Exeunt.
                [Horns winded within.

   Enter Theseus, Hippolyta, Egeus, and train.

Theseus

    Go, one of you, find out the forester,
    For now our observation is perform'd;
    And since we have the vaward of the day,   105
    My love shall hear the music of my hounds.
    Uncouple in the western valley; let them go.
    Dispatch, I say, and find the forester.

                  [Exit an Attendant.
    We will, fair queen, up to the mountain's top,
    And mark the musical confusion   110
    Of hounds and echo in conjunction.

Hippolyta

    I was with Hercules and Cadmus once,
    When in a wood of Crete they bay'd the bear
    With hounds of Sparta. Never did I hear
    Such gallant chiding. For, besides the groves,   115
    The skies, the fountains, every region near
    Seem'd all one mutual cry. I never heard
    So musical a discord, such sweet thunder.

Theseus

    My hounds are bred out of the Spartan kind,
    So flew'd, so sanded; and their heads are hung 120
    With ears that sweep away the morning dew;
    Crook-knee'd, and dew-lapp'd like Thessalian bulls;
    Slow in pursuit, but match'd in mouth like bells,

124 **tuneable** melodious

127 **soft!** stop!

131 **of** at

134 **in grace ... solemnity** to do honor to our festivity

138 **within** offstage

139 **Saint Valentine** birds, it was believed, chose their mates on St. Valentine's day

144 **concord** harmony
145 **jealousy** suspicion
146 **To sleep by hate** to sleep alongside an enemy

147 **amazedly** as a confused person

Each under each. A cry more tuneable
Was never holla'd to, nor cheer'd with horn,   125
In Crete, in Sparta, nor in Thessaly.
Judge when you hear. But, soft! What nymphs are
        these?

Egeus

My lord, this is my daughter here asleep;
And this, Lysander; this Demetrius is;
This Helena, old Nedar's Helena.   130
I wonder of their being here together.

Theseus

No doubt they rose up early to observe
The rite of May; and, hearing our intent,
Came here in grace of our solemnity.
But speak, Egeus. Is not this the day   135
That Hermia should give answer of her choice?

Egeus

It is, my lord.

Theseus

Go, bid the huntsmen awake them with their horns.
        [*Horns and shout within. Lysander, Demetrius,
                Helena, and Hermia wake and start up.*
Good morrow, friends. Saint Valentine is past.
Begin these wood birds but to couple now?   140

Lysander

Pardon, my lord.

Theseus

                        I pray you all, stand up.
I know you two are rival enemies.
How comes this gentle concord in the world,
That hatred is so far from jealousy,   145
To sleep by hate, and fear no enmity?

Lysander

My lord, I shall reply amazedly,
Half sleep, half waking. But as yet, I swear,

153 **where we might** wherever we could
154 **Without** outside of

155 **Enough** proof enough of your guilt

158 **defeated** defrauded

161 **stealth** stealing away

164 **fancy** love
165 **wot** know

168 **an idle gaud** a foolish trinket

174 **like in sickness** like one who is sick
175 **come** having come back

I cannot truly say how I came here.
But, as I think—for truly would I speak,   150
And now I do bethink me, so it is—
I came with Hermia hither. Our intent
Was to be gone from Athens, where we might,
Without the peril of the Athenian law.

Egeus

Enough, enough, my lord; you have enough.   155
I beg the law, the law, upon his head.
They would have stolen away. They would,
    Demetrius,
Thereby to have defeated you and me,
You of your wife and me of my consent,
Of my consent that she should be your wife.   160

Demetrius

My lord, fair Helen told me of their stealth,
Of this their purpose hither to this wood;
And I in fury hither follow'd them,
Fair Helena in fancy following me.
But, my good lord, I wot not by what power—   165
But by some power it is—my love to Hermia,
Melted as the snow, seems to me now
As the remembrance of an idle gaud,
Which in my childhood I did dote upon.
And all the faith, the virtue of my heart,   170
The object and the pleasure of mine eye,
Is only Helena. To her, my lord,
Was I betroth'd ere I saw Hermia.
But, like in sickness, did I loathe this food;
But, as in health, come to my natural taste,   175
Now I do wish it, love it, long for it,
And will for evermore be true to it.

Theseus

Fair lovers, you are fortunately met.
Of this discourse we more will hear anon.

180 **overbear** overrule
181 **by and by** immediately

183 **for** since

190 **with parted eye** with divided vision; out of focus

193 **like . . . own** like a precious thing found by chance, not mine but in my possession

203 **recount** tell each other about

Egeus, I will overbear your will,   180
For in the temple, by and by, with us
These couples shall eternally be knit.
And, for the morning now is something worn,
Our purposed hunting shall be set aside.
Away with us to Athens! Three and three,   185
We'll hold a feast in great solemnity.
Come, Hippolyta.
                    [*Exeunt Theseus, Hippolyta, and train.*

Demetrius
These things seem small and undistinguishable,
Like far-off mountains turned into clouds.

Hermia
Methinks I see these things with parted eye,   190
When everything seems double.

Helena
                              So methinks.
And I have found Demetrius like a jewel,
Mine own, and not mine own.

Demetrius
                              Are you sure   195
That we are awake? It seems to me
That yet we sleep, we dream. Do not you think
The Duke was here, and bid us follow him?

Hermia
Yea, and my father.

Helena
                    And Hippolyta.   200

Lysander
And he did bid us follow to the temple.

Demetrius
Why, then, we are awake. Let's follow him,
And by the way let us recount our dreams.
                                        [*Exeunt.*

205 **Heigh-ho!** (yawns)

207 **God's my life** God save my life

210 **go about** attempt

213 **patched** suggest a jester's multicolored clothes

218 **ballad** ballet
219 **hath no bottom** is all tangled up because it has no
core

222 **gracious** attractive
her refers to Thisby

4 **transported** carried off by fairies

Bottom

[*Awaking*] When my cue comes, call me, and I will
answer. My next is, "Most fair Pyramus." Heigh-ho!   205
Peter Quince! Flute, the bellows mender! Snout, the
tinker! Starveling! God's my life, stolen hence, and
left me asleep! I have had a most rare vision. I have
had a dream, past the wit of a man to say what dream
it was. Man is but an ass, if he go about to expound   210
this dream. Methought I was—there is no man can
tell what. Methought I was—and methought I had—
but man is but a patched fool, if he will offer to say
what methought I had. The eye of man hath not
heard, the ear of man hath not seen, man's hand is   215
not able to taste, his tongue to conceive, nor his
heart to report, what my dream was. I will get Peter
Quince to write a ballad of this dream. It shall be
called Bottom's Dream, because it hath no bottom;
and I will sing it in the latter end of a play, before   220
the Duke. Peradventure, to make it the more
gracious, I shall sing it at her death.

[*Exit.*

Scene 2. Athens. Quince's house

Enter Quince, Flute, Snout, and Starveling.

Quince

Have you sent to Bottom's house? Is he come home
yet?

Starveling

He cannot be heard of. Out of doubt he is
transported.

8 discharge Pyramus do the job of playing Pyramus

9 wit understanding

13 paramour illicit lover
14 a thing of naught an evil thing

17 made men men whose fortunes have been made

19 sixpence as a royal pension

25 these hearts these fine fellows

26 courageous auspicious; favorable

27 I am to I have to
   discourse tell about

Flute

    If he come not, then the play is marred. It goes not   5
forward, doth it?

Quince

    It is not possible. You have not a man in all Athens
able to discharge Pyramus but he.

Flute

    No, he hath simply the best wit of any handicraft
man in Athens.   10

Quince

    Yea, and the best person too, and he is a very
paramour for a sweet voice.

Flute

    You must say "paragon." A paramour is, God bless
us, a thing of naught.

    Enter Snug.

Snug

    Masters, the Duke is coming from the temple, and   15
there is two or three lords and ladies more married.
If our sport had gone forward, we had all been made
men.

Flute

    O sweet bully Bottom! Thus hath he lost sixpence a
day during his life. He could not have scaped   20
sixpence a day. An the Duke had not given him
sixpence a day for playing Pyramus, I'll be hanged.
He would have deserved it. Sixpence a day in
Pyramus, or nothing.

    Enter Bottom.

Bottom

    Where are these lads? Where are these hearts?   25

Quince

    Bottom! O most courageous day! O most happy hour!

Bottom

    Masters, I am to discourse wonders, but ask me not

29 right exactly

31 of from

33 strings (used to attach false beards)
34 presently instantly

36 preferred recommended

what. For if I tell you, I am no true Athenian. I will
tell you everything, right as it fell out.

Quince

Let us hear, sweet Bottom.   30

Bottom

Not a word of me. All that I will tell you is, that the
Duke hath dined. Get your apparel together, good
strings to your beards, new ribbons to your pumps.
Meet presently at the palace. Every man look o'er
his part, for the short and the long is, our play is   35
preferred. In any case, let Thisby have clean linen,
and let not him that plays the lion pare his nails, for
they shall hang out for the lion's claws. And, most
dear actors, eat no onions nor garlic, for we are to
utter sweet breath. And I do not doubt but to hear   40
them say, it is a sweet comedy. No more words.
Away! Go, away!

[Exeunt.

1 **that** what

2 **may** can
3 **toys** foolish stories; trifles
4 **seething** boiling
5 **fantasies** imaginations
6 **comprehends** takes to be reasonable

8 **compact** composed

11 **a brow of Egypt** a gypsy's face. Only blondes were thought beautiful by the Elizabethans.

19 **would but** merely wishes to
20 **comprehends** takes in
21 **fear** object of fear

ACT V

Enter Theseus, Hippolyta, Philostrate, Lords, and Attendants.

Hippolyta
'Tis strange, my Theseus, that these lovers speak of.
Theseus
   More strange than true. I never may believe
   These antique fables, nor these fairy toys.
   Lovers and madmen have such seething brains,
   Such shaping fantasies, that apprehend   5
   More than cool reason ever comprehends.
   The lunatic, the lover, and the poet
   Are of imagination all compact.
   One sees more devils than vast hell can hold,
   That is the madman. The lover, all as frantic,   10
   Sees Helen's beauty in a brow of Egypt.
   The poet's eye, in a fine frenzy rolling,
   Doth glance from heaven to earth, from earth to heaven;
   And as imagination bodies forth
   The forms of things unknown, the poet's pen   15
   Turns them to shapes, and gives to airy nothing
   A local habitation and a name.
   Such tricks hath strong imagination,
   That, if it would but apprehend some joy,
   It comprehends some bringer of that joy;   20
   Or in the night, imagining some fear,
   How easy is a bush supposed a bear!

25 **More witnesseth**   gives evidence of more
   fancy's images   ideas created by the imagination
26 **constancy**   consistency
27 **admirable**   wonderful

31 **More**   more joy

35 **aftersupper**   a light meal served after the usual evening meal
36 **mirth**   entertainment

41 **abridgment**   pastime (to make the evening seem
   shorter)

44 **brief**   written list
   ripe   ready for presentation

Hippolyta
  But all the story of the night told over,
  And all their minds transfigured so together,
  More witnesseth than fancy's images   25
  And grows to something of great constancy;
  But, howsoever, strange and admirable.
Theseus
  Here come the lovers, full of joy and mirth.

    Enter Lysander, Demetrius, Hermia, and Helena.

  Joy, gentle friends! Joy and fresh days of love
  Accompany your hearts!   30
Lysander
                    More than to us
  Wait in your royal walks, your board, your bed!
Theseus
  Come now, what masques, what dances shall we
      have,
  To wear away this long age of three hours
  Between our aftersupper and bedtime?   35
  Where is our usual manager of mirth?
  What revels are in hand? Is there no play,
  To ease the anguish of a torturing hour?
  Call Philostrate.
Philostrate
                    Here, mighty Theseus.   40
Theseus
  Say, what abridgment have you for this evening?
  What masque? What music? How shall we beguile
  The lazy time, if not with some delight?
Philostrate
  There is a brief how many sports are ripe.
  Make choice of which your highness will see first.   45
                              [*Giving a paper.*
Theseus
  [*Reads*] The battle with the Centaurs, to be sung
  By an Athenian eunuch to the harp.

We'll none of that. That have I told my love,
In glory of my kinsman Hercules.
[*Reads*]   The riot of the tipsy Bacchanals,   50
Tearing the Thracian singer in their rage.
That is an old device, and it was play'd
When I from Thebes came last a conqueror.
[*Reads*]   The thrice three Muses mourning for the
      death
Of Learning, late deceased in beggary.   55
That is some satire, keen and critical,
Not sorting with a nuptial ceremony.
[*Reads*]   A tedious brief scene of young Pyramus
And his love Thisby; very tragical mirth.
Merry and tragical! Tedious and brief!   60
That is, hot ice and wondrous strange snow.
How shall we find the concord of this discord?

Philostrate

A play there is, my lord, some ten words long,
Which, is as brief as I have known a play;
But by ten words, my lord, it is too long,   65
Which makes it tedious. For in all the play
There is not one word apt, one player fitted.
And tragical, my noble lord, it is;
For Pyramus therein doth kill himself.
Which, when I saw rehearsed, I must confess,   70
Made mine eyes water; but more merry tears
The passion of loud laughter never shed.

Theseus

What are they that do play it?

Philostrate

Hard-handed men, that work in Athens here,
Which never labor'd in their minds till now;   75
And now have toil'd their unbreathed memories
With this same play, against your nuptial.

Theseus

And we will hear it.

83 **stretch'd** strained
   conn'd learned by heart

87 **simpleness** sincerity

89 **wretchedness o'ercharged** poor overburdened creatures
90 **duty . . . perishing** devoted effort ruining itself

94 **sport** enjoyment (we accept their mistaken effort to
   please us)
95 **And what . . . merit** we consider their ability and not
   the merit of their performance
97 **Where I have come** in different places I have been
   to
   clerks men of learning
100 **periods** long stops
101 **Throttle . . . fears** permit their fears to choke their
   well-trained delivery

109 **In least** the less they say, the more they really express
   to my capacity as I can understand it

Philostrate
                    No, my noble lord,
It is not for you. I have heard it over,   80
And it is nothing, nothing in the world;
Unless you can find sport in their intents,
Extremely stretch'd and conn'd with cruel pain,
To do you service.

Theseus
                    I will hear that play;   85
For never anything can be amiss,
When simpleness and duty tender it.
Go, bring them in, and take your places, ladies.

                              [*Exit Philostrate.*

Hippolyta
I love not to see wretchedness o'ercharged,
And duty in his service perishing.   90

Theseus
Why, gentle sweet, you shall see no such thing.

Hippolyta
He says they can do nothing in this kind.

Theseus
The kinder we, to give them thanks for nothing.
Our sport shall be to take what they mistake.
And what poor duty cannot do, noble respect   95
Takes it in might, not merit.
Where I have come, great clerks have purposed
To greet me with premeditated welcomes;
Where I have seen them shiver and look pale,
Make periods in the midst of sentences,   100
Throttle their practiced accent in their fears,
And, in conclusion, dumbly have broke off,
Not paying me a welcome. Trust me, sweet,
Out of this silence yet I picked a welcome;
And in the modesty of fearful duty   105
I read as much as from the rattling tongue
Of saucy and audacious eloquence.
Love, therefore, and tongue-tied simplicity
In least speak most, to my capacity.

110 **The Prologue is address'd** the speaker of the Prologue is ready

112 **If we offend . . . are like to know** The prologue is punctuated incorrectly, making it comical nonsense.

122 **doth . . . points** pays no attention to marks of punctuation
123 **rough** untrained
124 **stop** mark of punctuation
125 **true** correctly

127 **recorder** musical instrument, like a flute
    government good management
128 **nothing impaired** not at all broken

130 **Gentles** gentlemen and ladies

Reenter Philostrate.

Philostrate
  So please your grace, the Prologue is address'd.   110
Theseus
  Let him approach.

                           [*Flourish of trumpets.*

  Enter Quince for the Prologue.

Prologue
  If we offend, it is with our goodwill.
  That you should think, we come not to offend,
  But with goodwill. To show our simple skill,
  That is the true beginning of our end.   115
  Consider, then, we come but in despite.
  We do not come, as minding to content you,
  Our true intent is. All for your delight,
  We are not here. That you should here repent you,
  The actors are at hand; and, by their show,   120
  You shall know all, that you are like to know.
Theseus
  This fellow doth not stand upon points.
Lysander
  He hath rid his prologue like a rough colt; he knows
  not the stop. A good moral, my lord: it is not enough
  to speak, but to speak true.   125
Hippolyta
  Indeed he hath played on his prologue like a child
  on a recorder—a sound, but not in government.
Theseus
  His speech was like a tangled chain: nothing
  impaired, but all disordered. Who is next?

  *Enter Pyramus and Thisby, Wall, Moonshine, and
  Lion.*

Prologue
  Gentles, perchance you wonder at this show;   130
  But wonder on, till truth make all things plain.

134 **present** impersonate
135 **sunder** break apart

140 **did . . . think no scorn** did not regard it as a disgrace

142 **hight** is named

145 **fall** let fall

147 **tall** brave

149 **Whereat . . . breast** check *alliteration* in your dictionary. Shakespeare is poking fun at contemporary poets
150 **broach'd** pierced; stabbed

154 **At large** at full length

156 **No wonder** it will be no wonder if he does

157 **interlude** short play

This man is Pyramus, if you would know;
This beauteous lady Thisby is certain.
This man, with lime and roughcast, doth present
Wall, that vile Wall which did these lovers sunder.   135
And through Wall's chink, poor souls, they are
    content
To whisper. At the which let no man wonder.
This man, with lantern, dog, and bush of thorn,
Presenteth Moonshine. For, if you will know,
By moonshine did these lovers think no scorn   140
To meet at Ninus' tomb, there, there to woo.
This grisly beast, which Lion hight by name,
The trusty Thisby, coming first by night,
Did scare away, or rather did affright;
And, as she fled, her mantle she did fall,   145
Which Lion vile with bloody mouth did stain.
Anon comes Pyramus, sweet youth and tall,
And finds his trusty Thisby's mantle slain;
Whereat, with blade, with bloody blameful blade,
He bravely broach'd his boiling bloody breast.   150
And Thisby, tarrying in mulberry shade,
His dagger drew, and died. For all the rest,
Let Lion, Moonshine, Wall, and lovers twain
At large discourse, while here they do remain.
      [*Exeunt Prologue, Pyramus, Thisby, Lion, and*
                      Moonshine.

Theseus
  I wonder if the lion be to speak.   155
Demetrius
  No wonder, my lord. One lion may, when many asses
    do.
Wall
  In this same interlude it doth befall
  That I, one Snout by name, present a wall;
  And such a wall, as I would have you think,
  That had in it a crannied hole or chink,   160
  Through which the lovers, Pyramus and Thisby,

165 **cranny** opening
   right and sinister right and left
166 **fearful** timid

168 **wittiest** most intelligent

170 **grim-look'd** grim-faced

182 **being sensible** having the feelings and mind of a human being

186 **fall pat as** happen exactly as

Did whisper often very secretly.
This loam, this roughcast, and this stone, doth show
That I am that same wall. The truth is so.
And this the cranny is, right and sinister,   165
Through which the fearful lovers are to whisper.

Theseus
Would you desire lime and hair to speak better?

Demetrius
It is the wittiest partition that ever I heard discourse,
    my lord.

Theseus
Pyramus draws near the wall. Silence!

    Reenter Pyramus.

Pyramus
O grim-look'd night! O night with hue so black!   170
O night, which ever art when day is not!
O night, O night! Alack, alack, alack,
I fear my Thisby's promise is forgot!
And thou, O wall, O sweet, O lovely wall,
That stand'st between her father's ground and mine!   175
Thou wall, O wall, O sweet and lovely wall,
Show me thy chink, to blink through with mine eyne!
                              [*Wall holds up his fingers.*
Thanks, courteous wall. Jove shield thee well for this!
But what see I? No Thisby do I see.
O wicked wall, through whom I see no bliss!   180
Cursed be thy stones for thus deceiving me!

Theseus
The wall, methinks, being sensible, should curse
again.

Pyramus
No, in truth, sir, he should not. "Deceiving me" is
Thisby's cue. She is to enter now, and I am to spy   185
her through the wall. You shall see, it will fall pat as
I told you. Yonder she comes.

196 **grace** beautiful self
197 **Limander** blunder for Leander
   still always
198 **Helen** actor means Hero

199 **Shafalus to Procrus** Cephalus to Procris

204 **Tide . . . death** whether life or death takes place

205 **discharged** performed

207 **mural** wall

Reenter Thisby.

Thisby
   O wall, full often hast thou heard my moans,
   For parting my fair Pyramus and me!
   My cherry lips have often kiss'd thy stones,   190
   Thy stones with lime and hair knit up in thee.

Pyramus
   I see a voice. Now will I to the chink,
   To spy an I can hear my Thisby's face.
   Thisby!

Thisby
   My love! Thou art my love, I think.   195

Pyramus
   Think what thou wilt, I am thy lover's grace;
   And, like Limander, am I trusty still.

Thisby
   And I, like Helen, till the Fates me kill.

Pyramus
   Not Shafalus to Procrus was so true.

Thisby
   As Shafalus to Procrus, I to you.   200

Pyramus
   O, kiss me through the hole of this vile wall!

Thisby
   I kiss the wall's hole, not your lips at all.

Pyramus
   Wilt thou at Ninny's tomb meet me straightway?

Thisby
   'Tide life, 'tide death, I come without delay.
                       [Exeunt Pyramus and Thisby.

Wall
   Thus have I, Wall, my part discharged so;   205
   And, being done, thus Wall away doth go.
                             [Exit.

Theseus
   Now is the mural down between the two neighbors.

211 **best** best plays

222 **A lion fell** neither a fierce lion nor a lioness

224 **'twere pity on my life** I should be in danger of hang-
ing
225 **gentle** polite

227 **This lion ... for his valor** he is more crafty than brave

228 **a goose** more foolish than crafty

Demetrius
No remedy, my lord, when walls are so willful to hear
without warning.

Hippolyta
This is the silliest stuff that ever I heard. 210

Theseus
The best in this kind are but shadows; and the worst
are no worse, if imagination amend them.

Hippolyta
It must be your imagination then, and not theirs.

Theseus
If we imagine no worse of them than they of
themselves, they may pass for excellent men. Here 215
come two noble beasts in, a man and a lion.

Reenter Lion and Moonshine.

Lion
You, ladies, you, whose gentle hearts do fear
The smallest monstrous mouse that creeps on floor,
May now perchance both quake and tremble here,
When lion rough in wildest rage doth roar, 220
Then know that I, one Snug the joiner, am
A lion fell, nor else no lion's dam.
For, if I should as lion come in strife
Into this place, 'twere pity on my life.

Theseus
A very gentle beast, and of a good conscience. 225

Demetrius
The very best at a beast, my lord, that e'er I saw.

Lysander
This lion is a very fox for his valor.

Theseus
True. And a goose for his discretion.

Demetrius
Not so, my lord. For his valor cannot carry his
discretion, and the fox carries the goose. 230

235 He . . . head   This is an old joke about the horns of
a cuckold

243 for the candle   on account of the candle
244 in snuff   in need of snuffing; offended

248 stay the time   see it through

Theseus

His discretion, I am sure, cannot carry his valor; for
the goose carries not the fox. It is well. Leave it to
his discretion, and let us listen to the moon.

Moonshine

This lantern doth the horned moon present—

Demetrius

He should have worn the horns on his head.   235

Theseus

He is no crescent, and his horns are invisible within
the circumference.

Moonshine

This lantern doth the horned moon present.
Myself the man i' the moon do seem to be.

Theseus

This is the greatest error of all the rest. The man   240
should be put into the lantern. How is it else the
man i' the moon?

Demetrius

He dares not come there for the candle; for, you see,
it is already in snuff.

Hippolyta

I am aweary of this moon. Would he would change!   245

Theseus

It appears, by his small light of discretion, that he is
in the wane; but yet, in courtesy, in all reason, we
must stay the time.

Lysander

Proceed, Moon.

Moonshine

All that I have to say is to tell you that the lantern   250
is the moon; I, the man i' the moon; this thorn-bush,
my thorn-bush; and this dog, my dog.

Demetrius

Why, all these should be in the lantern; for all these
are in the moon. But, silence! Here comes Thisby.

261 moused shaken; torn (like a mouse in a cat's jaws)

268 spite! disaster

270 dole sorrow

276 fell fierce

Reenter Thisby.

Thisby
This is old Ninny's tomb. Where is my love?   255
Lion
[*Roaring*]   Oh—

                                        [*Thisby runs off.*

Demetrius
Well roared, Lion.
Theseus
Well run, Thisby.
Hippolyta
Well shone, Moon. Truly, the moon shines with a
good grace.   260

          [*The Lion shakes Thisby's mantle, and exit.*

Theseus
Well moused, Lion.
Demetrius
And then came Pyramus.
Lysander
And so the lion vanished.

     Reenter Pyramus.

Pyramus
Sweet Moon, I thank thee for thy sunny beams;
I thank thee, Moon, for shining now so bright;   265
For, by thy gracious, golden, glittering gleams,
I trust to take of truest Thisby sight.
          But stay, O spite!
          But mark, poor knight,
What dreadful dole is here!   270
          Eyes, do you see?
          How can it be?
O dainty duck! O dear!
          Thy mantle good,
          What, stain'd with blood!   275
Approach, ye Furies fell!

278 **thrum**   the whole thread of life
279 **Quail**   subdue; overpower
    quell   kill

281 **go near to**   almost

282 **Beshrew**   curse

284 **deflower'd**   ravished

288 **confound**   destroy me

290 **pap**   nipple

297 **Tongue . . . light**   be made dumb by death
298 **Moon . . . flight**   get off the stage

299 **die**   (pun) 1. to pass away and 2. singular of dice.

300 **one**   in a class by himself

301 **ace**   a one on a die (singular for dice)

  O Fates, come, come,
  Cut thread and thrum;
 Quail, crush, conclude, and quell!

Theseus

 This passion, and the death of a dear friend, would 280
 go near to make a man look sad.

Hippolyta

 Beshrew my heart, but I pity the man.

Pyramus

 O wherefore, Nature, didst thou lions frame?
 Since lion vile hath here deflower'd my dear;
 Which is—no, no—which was the fairest dame 285
 That lived, that loved, that liked, that look'd with
   cheer.
   Come, tears, confound!
   Out, sword, and wound
 The pap of Pyramus! 290
   Ay, that left pap,
   Where heart doth hop.

          [Stabs himself.

 Thus die I, thus, thus, thus.
   Now am I dead,
   Now am I fled; 295
 My soul is in the sky.
   Tongue, lose thy light;
   Moon, take thy flight.

         [Exit Moonshine.

 Now die, die, die, die, die!

           [Dies.

Demetrius

 No die, but an ace, for him; for he is but one. 300

Lysander

 Less than an ace, man; for he is dead, he is nothing.

Theseus

 With the help of a surgeon he might yet recover,
 and prove an ass.

304 **How chance** how does it happen that

307 **passion** expression of grief

310 **mote** speck of dust
311 **God warrant us** God protect us (an expression used
   to repel an evil omen)

314 **means** moans
   videlicet as follows

327 **Sisters Three** the Fates

Hippolyta

How chance Moonshine is gone before Thisby comes
back and finds her lover?   305

Theseus

She will find him by starlight. Here she comes; and
her passion ends the play.

Reenter Thisby.

Hippolyta

Methinks she should not use a long one for such a
Pyramus. I hope she will be brief.

Demetrius

A mote will turn the balance, which Pyramus, which   310
Thisby, is the better; he for a man, God warrant us;
she for a woman, God bless us.

Lysander

She hath spied him already with those sweet eyes.

Demetrius

And thus she means, videlicet:

Thisby

        Asleep, my love?   315
        What, dead, my dove?
     O Pyramus, arise!
        Speak, speak. Quite dumb?
        Dead, dead? A tomb
   Must cover thy sweet eyes.   320
        These lily lips,
        This cherry nose,
   These yellow cowslip cheeks,
        Are gone, are gone.
        Lovers, make moan!   325
   His eyes were green as leeks.
        O Sisters Three,
        Come, come to me,
   With hands as pale as milk:
        Lay them in gore,   330
        Since you have shore

335 **imbrue** stain with blood

343 **Bergomask** country dance from Bergamo in Italy

345 **no excuse** no apology for its faults

350 **discharged** performed

352 **told** struck
353 **fairy time** from midnight until dawn

355 **overwatch'd** stayed up too late
356 **palpable gross** obviously stupid
357 **heavy** slow-paced; dull

>   With shears his thread of silk.
>   Tongue, not a word.
>   Come, trusty sword,
>   Come, blade, my breast imbrue!   335
>   [*Stabs herself.*
>   And, farewell, friends.
>   Thus Thisby ends.
>   Adieu, adieu, adieu!
>   [*Dies.*

Theseus

Moonshine and Lion are left to bury the dead.

Demetrius

Ay, and Wall too.   340

Bottom

[*Starting up*] No, I assure you; the wall is down that
parted their fathers. Will it please you to see the
epilogue, or to hear a Bergomask dance between two
of our company?

Theseus

No epilogue, I pray you, for your play needs no   345
excuse. Never excuse, for when the players are all
dead, there need none to be blamed. Marry, if he
that writ it had played Pyramus and hanged himself
in Thisby's garter, it would have been a fine tragedy.
And so it is truly, and very notably discharged. But,   350
come, your Bergomask. Let your epilogue alone.
                                   [*A dance.*
The iron tongue of midnight hath told twelve.
Lovers, to bed; 'tis almost fairy time.
I fear we shall out-sleep the coming morn,
As much as we this night have overwatch'd.   355
This palpable gross play hath well beguiled
The heavy gait of night. Sweet friends, to bed.
A fortnight hold we this solemnity,
In nightly revels and new jollity.
                                   [*Exeunt.*

Enter Puck.

362 **heavy**   dull with sleep
363 **fordone**   exhausted
364 **brands**   logs burned to embers
365 **owl**   bird of ill-omen

370 **sprite**   fairy; ghost

373 **triple Hecate**   The moon goddess had three names: Diana on earth, Phoebe in heaven, and Hecate in Hades. Here she is queen of night, drawn by her team of dragons.
376 **frolic**   merry

379 **behind**   from behind (Puck helped clean the house of the king and queen)

Puck

 Now the hungry lion roars,   360
  And the wolf behowls the moon;
 Whilst the heavy plowman snores,
  All with weary task fordone.
 Now the wasted brands do glow,
  Whilst the screech owl, screeching loud, 365
 Puts the wretch that lies in woe
  In remembrance of a shroud.
 Now it is the time of night
  That the graves, all gaping wide,
 Every one lets forth his sprite,   370
  In the churchway paths to glide.
 And we fairies, that do run
  By the triple Hecate's team,
 From the presence of the sun,
  Following darkness like a dream,   375
 Now are frolic. Not a mouse
 Shall disturb this hallow'd house.
 I am sent with broom before,
 To sweep the dust behind the door.

  Enter Oberon and Titania with their train.

Oberon

 Through the house give glimmering light, 380
  By the dead and drowsy fire.
 Every elf and fairy sprite
  Hop as light as bird from brier;
 And this ditty, after me,
 Sing, and dance it trippingly.   385

Titania

 First, rehearse your song by rote,
 To each word a warbling note.
 Hand in hand, with fairy grace,
 Will we sing, and bless this place.
        [Song and dance.

Oberon

 Now, until the break of day,   390
 Through this house each fairy stray.

394 **create** created

398 **blots** ugly natural blemishes

401 **mark prodigious** abnormal birthmark, showing bad luck
402 **nativity** birth
404 **consecrate** holy
405 **take his gait** make his way
406 **several** separate

414 **That . . . here** that it is only "a midsummer night's dream"
416 **idle** foolish
417 **No more** yielding nothing more than
418 **Gentles** ladies and gentlemen
419 **mend** do better the next time

422 **the serpent's tongue** hisses from the audience

426 **your hands** in applause
427 **restore amends** improve the play to make up for all its defects

To the best bride-bed will we,
Which by us shall blessed be;
And the issue there create
Ever shall be fortunate.   395
So shall all the couples three
Ever true in loving be;
And the blots of Nature's hand
Shall not in their issue stand;
Never mole, harelip, nor scar,   400
Nor mark prodigious, such as are
Despised in nativity,
Shall upon their children be.
With this field-dew consecrate,
Every fairy take his gait;   405
And each several chamber bless,
Through this palace, with sweet peace,
And the owner of it blest
Ever shall in safety rest.
Trip away; make no stay;   410
Meet me all by break of day.
                    [*Exeunt Oberon, Titania, and train.*

Puck
If we shadows have offended,
Think but this, and all is mended,
That you have but slumber'd here,
While these visions did appear.   415
And this weak and idle theme,
No more yielding but a dream,
Gentles, do not reprehend.
If you pardon, we will mend.
And, as I am an honest Puck,   420
If we have unearned luck
Now to scape the serpent's tongue,
We will make amends ere long;
Else the Puck a liar call.
So, good night unto you all.   425
Give me your hands, if we be friends,
And Robin shall restore amends.

                                        [*Exit.*

READER'S GUIDE

Abraham Poneman

INTRODUCTION

A midsummer night. Magic. Young lovers try to escape the harsh judgments of the world. Into the woods they flee, joining a world of spirits, of night creatures that fly about swiftly until dawn and disappear with the first rays of morning light.

Do the woods offer solace, comfort, healing—the fulfillment of young dreams? Not at all. There are deliberate deceptions perpetrated by these airy spirits. As a result, there is turmoil, confusion, misunderstanding. Lovers quarrel. They revile one another, turning love into hate. Young love seems fickle and perverse. Is this the normal order of things or are young lovers inevitably to be victims of a midsummer night? When at dawn all is set right again, were the confusion and hate just a bad dream in the darkness of night, a horror to be reversed when eyes opened again to light? Are the magic juices on the lovers' eyelids merely symbols of the bad dream that distort reality for a while when we close our eyes and subconsciously turn our lives upside down until we awaken again?

But this play is about more than dreams and awakening. It is also an experience, as are all of Shakespeare's plays, with the world of the playwright—his imagination, his sensory responses, his language, his artistry in defining for us what lacks clarity and definition without his intervention.

Darkness to Shakespeare has jaws that devour both heaven and earth, removing them from our sight. Dew on a blade of grass is a liquid pearl. At night, waiting to disturb us, are snakes, hedgehogs, newts, blindworms, spiders, beetles, snails, cats, bears, leopards, and boars. In the world of darkness, lions roar, wolves howl, workers snore, logs burn to embers, the screech owl screeches, and fairies emerge from graves to glide through churchyards and to frolic. Fairies, those tiny elves, wander everywhere at night, move swiftly, serve the fairy Queen, place dew on the grass, and guard flowers.

We learn from Shakespeare that a mermaid can ride on a dolphin's back, sing sweetly, calm a rough sea, and make stars shoot madly from their spheres. He tells us, too, that quarrels between important people can disturb nature. They make winds bring fog. Rivers overflow. Crops rot. Cattle drown. Crows eat

169

bodies of dead cattle. Familiar paths disappear. Playing fields become too muddy for sport. Diseases abound—the seasons alter, with winter ice killing summer buds so that people can't tell one season from another.

If Shakespeare wants to take us to a special place in the woods, he shows us what grows there: wild thyme, oxlips, violets, woodbine, musk rose, and eglantine. If fairies serve you, they give you jewels, arrange for you to sleep on pressed flowers, feed you fruit and honey, light your way at night, fan moonbeams from your sleeping eyes, and attend you when you get up and when you get to bed. If you and a good friend have grown up together, you are like two cherries on the same stem.

To help you see all of this—and more—the Reader's Guide is organized to follow six strands for each act and scene of the play. These are:

> Reading Comprehension
> Characterization
> Style and Language
> Human Relations
> Comparisons with Modern Life
> Speak and Listen: Reading Aloud, Dramatization

READING COMPREHENSION

At times some teachers assign a play of Shakespeare's for home reading. They offer no guidance. Students are left to their own resources. Presumably some students are very resourceful. They find an edition with ample notes. They use ordinary and classical dictionaries. They are good readers to begin with.

Most high school students, however, even those considered superior readers, can profit from guidance in reading comprehension and in the five other strands reappearing throughout this Reader's Guide. Most readers cannot read Shakespeare as they do the daily newspaper. Shakespeare wrote about four centuries ago. His was a world without radio, TV, electricity, modern plumbing, automobiles, airplanes, and packaged food. Daily life and routines among his contemporaries were much different from what they are today—and language was different too. It is to bridge the gap between Shakespeare's day and ours that a Reader's Guide can be almost indispensable. This edition, therefore, offers two kinds of help:

1. Facing pages in the text itself explain words, phrases, and lines likely to need clarification.
2. Questions in the Reading Comprehension section of the Guide challenge your ability to follow what is happening in the play. Page and line references after each question guide you as you seek the correct answer. Subsequently, through class discussion or when your teacher reviews the answers with you, you'll be able to judge your success in finding a correct response.

These guide questions will help you look for and see much that you might otherwise overlook. They will help you follow feelings, motives, characterization, attitudes, aspects of Athenian life, conflicts, and the movement of the story. There are questions calling for interpretation, stimulating controversy, eliciting comparisons between life then and now, encouraging you to examine human relations, and enabling some of you to become "ham" actors through oral reading and participation in the dramatic presentation of selected scenes. In addition, one whole strand is devoted exclusively to Shakespeare's style and language.

If you pursue conscientiously the questions in the Reading Comprehension strand, you will understand the play. Your achievement will be much deeper and much more rewarding than that of the student who has been left to his own resources.

CHARACTERIZATION

A Midsummer Night's Dream is a comedy. In it we do not find the profound and moving characterizations present in *Hamlet, Macbeth, Othello,* and *King Lear.* The settings, the comic antics, the horseplay, the woodland deceptions, the swift fairy movements of their night world, the songs, and the dancing tend to overshadow serious characterization. Nevertheless, there are some portraits, however thin, that we can discover.

The characterizations in this play do raise some questions for the alert reader. For example, is Theseus a stern ruler enforcing

harsh Athenian laws unimaginatively; or is he human and flexible, bending tolerantly and showing kindness when the oc-
casion calls for a generous gesture? Is Egeus, the tyrannical
father, worthy of our contemporary scorn, or is he merely the
victim of customs and traditions he has grown up with? Are the
young lovers individuals in their own right or are they merely
the puppets of love, being dangled and manipulated by a perverse stringmaster? Are they, in other words, in charge of their
fate, or are they merely examples of an ancient adage that "the
course of true love never did run smooth"? Are the quarrels of
Oberon and Titania a reflection in the fairy kingdom of the
normal friction between husband and wife in the world of mortals? Is Puck merely Robin Goodfellow of British legend, or is
he a perverse imp personifying malicious mischief associated
with a belief in goblins and hobgoblins? And the laborers turned
actors—are they actual portraits or merely satiric caricatures of
the Elizabethan stage Shakespeare knew so well, demonstrating
the good-natured ineptitude of the common man on the stage,
the rhetorical excesses in many contemporary plays, and the
declamatory ranting that some Elizabethan actors were so fond
of?

Specific line references in this strand direct you to passages
that help you judge the characters. At times you are encour-
aged to take pen in hand and make your assessment in writing.
This is a useful form of composition growing out of your study
of literature.

Your understanding of the characters will help you later when
you try oral interpretation of selected passages or when you
participate in rehearsing selected scenes for classroom dramatization.

STYLE AND LANGUAGE

Shakespeare is a poet. His style and language, therefore, reflect a poet's way of seeing the world. They illustrate, too, his
mastery of the poet's techniques for projecting his vision.

He uses a simile to show us that the moon is "like a silver
bow new bent in heaven." He uses metaphors when he describes dew on the grass as "liquid pearl" and tears as "a tem-

pest in the eyes." Allusions to "Cupid's best arrow," "Carthage queen," and "false Troyan" help invigorate his meanings. He uses alliteration satirically to poke fun at the rhetorical excesses in some of the plays of his contemporaries. In his prologue to the Pyramus and Thisby play, Quince anticipates the suicide of Pyramus by describing how the latter killed himself "with blade, with bloody, blameful blade/He bravely broached his boiling, bloody breast." Pyramus himself, dying, exclaims, "Quail, crush, conclude, and quell."

Shakespeare often uses precise words for their exact meaning; for example, *filched* (Act I, Scene 1, line 36), *leviathan* (II, 1, 174), and *girdle* (II, 1, 175).

In Shakespeare, the language used reflects the speaker's class. English laborers speak the colloquial Elizabethan prose of the common man. The upper classes speak in verse, even when they hurl vivid and vile epithets at one another. Confused laborers misuse words; for example, *paramour* for *paragon* and *odious* for *odors*. They also confuse names; for example, Hero and Leander become Helen and Limander. Quince pays no attention to punctuation marks as he reads his prologue.

Quotable lines abound:

The course of true love never did run smooth.

What fools these mortals be.

The lunatic, the lover, and the poet
Are of imagination all compact.

Shakespeare uses other techniques. His descriptions are full of appropriate and supporting details. He is fond of listings. For example, Oberon lists wild beasts. Hermia and Lysander list all obstacles that threaten true love. Egeus names love tokens: bracelets, rings, gawds, conceits, knacks, trifles, nosegays, sweetmeats. He likes to juxtapose opposites. Some examples are dream-waking, shadow-substance, imagination-reason, feigning-truth, anarchy-order, woods-city, fairy-mortal, night-day. Guide questions will direct your attention to other examples of these.

This Reader's Guide does not point to every example of Shakespeare's skill in using language. You will undoubtedly find additional examples not underscored by the questions.

HUMAN RELATIONS

Problems of human relations are universal. They emerge whenever people interact. The plays of Shakespeare are full of such interactions. A recent scholarly publication by Elizabeth Diane Dreher devotes a whole volume to such relationships, concentrating on fathers and daughters in the plays of Shakespeare. Her volume is called *Domination and Defiance—Fathers and Daughters in Shakespeare* (1986, University Press of Kentucky, Lexington, Kentucky).

The relationship of Egeus and Hermia is a prime example of Professor Dreher's theme of dominance and defiance. This is just one of many such instances. In *Shakespearean Comedy*, edited by Maurice Charney, there is a reference to what amounts to three stages of human relationships in society.

1. An "old" society imposes restrictive laws.
2. Confusion ensues.
3. Confusion is resolved through marriage. The result is a new society, with old people giving way to the fertile and vigorous young.

Helena complains that women "cannot fight for love as men may do." She admits: "We should be wooed and were not made to woo." Contemporary readers know that modern Helenas do not share her inhibitions.

The relationships of the young lovers in this play are probably controlled by Shakespeare's apparent theme that young love has no basis in reality. Shakespearean scholar Ernest Schanzer sees young love in this play as a "kind of madness, a dream, devoid of judgment. Love is wholly dependent on the whims of Cupid. Eyes are blinded, judgment is disabled, and reason put to flight." As Bottom says when Titania lovingly strokes his animal-head costume, "Reason and love keep little company nowadays."

Shakespeare floods this play with moonlight—and moonshine. When daylight comes, sanity returns and the dreaming ends.

More mature lovers, however, like Theseus and Hippolyta, are not subject to these irrational influences. They begin by setting a date for their wedding. Patiently they plan to endure the four days of painful waiting. They even plan carefully for the revelry and merriment to accompany and follow their wedding celebration.

Arranged marriages are not as common today as they used to be; but in China, India, parts of Europe, and here and there throughout the world, such marriages persist. The Guide encourages you to examine the advantages and disadvantages of this ancient custom.

In your discussions of human relations, you will doubtless examine rigidity vs. tolerance or flexibility among those in authority like Theseus. You may even touch upon the causes of friction between friends (Hermia and Helena). You'll want to examine the conflicts between husband and wife (Oberon and Titania). The next step, of course, is to consider remedies for the apparent discord.

When Bottom fails at first to show up for the final rehearsal of *Pyramus and Thisby,* his fellow actors show their respect and loyalty to him. They fear his absence is irreplaceable. The show cannot go on without him. His ultimate appearance fills them with genuine joy and relief. Thus do simple people have a way of showing their affection for one another.

COMPARISONS WITH MODERN LIFE

In a recent administration, a book by a White House official revealed that the first lady had consulted astrologers before allowing her husband, the president, to accept speaking engagements. The news was a sensation. Newspapers throughout the world featured the story.

Such an event would not have astonished Shakespeare's contemporaries. For them, consulting astrologers and fortune-tellers was a common way of predicting future possibilities. Natural disasters were traceable to a variety of causes. For example, quarrels between important people could lead to serious disturbances in nature.

Similarly, herbs and potions could produce miraculous effects—curing ailments, wiping out disease, and even making one fall madly in love with the first creature one saw after awakening. There is no lack of such "miracle" cures today.

You will be able to make many other comparisons between

your experiences today and those of the characters in *A Midsummer Night's Dream*. Fathers you know, like Egeus, may not approve of the friends of their children. They may choose to control every aspect of the life of their offspring. Perhaps at times you or your friends have defied your parents. Have you or a friend ever been responsible for mischief or deception that led to confusion or turmoil? Have you and a friend ever had a falling out, exchanging insults and turning a good relationship into a hostile one? Do some of your friends, thinking they are in love, actually, in your opinion, show poor judgment and a lack of reason in their choice of a partner?

Perhaps you have been involved in rehearsals for the production of a play—at camp, in school, or in your community. Have you met young would-be actors who think they should be the stars? Have you met others who have trouble learning their lines? If yes, your friends will remind you of those rehearsing *Pyramus and Thisby*.

The Reader's Guide will direct your attention to these possible comparisons between life then and now—and to many more.

SPEAK AND LISTEN: READING ALOUD

Reading memorable passages aloud can be a challenge for both the reader and the audience. See question 73 on page 183 of the Reader's Guide for instructions on selecting a passage and for preparing to present it to your class. Some of you will remember these passages long after your school days are over.

DRAMATIZATION

There are students who prefer this type of activity to almost anything else that happens during their school day. It allows them to work with others, to interact, to project their feelings, and to lose themselves in a characterization. See question 74 (page 184) for suggestions on how to proceed.

If you participate in the dramatic presentation of a selected scene from this play, you are likely to remember your experience for a long time.

QUESTIONS

Act I, Scenes 1 and 2

Summary (Scene 1) Theseus, Duke of Athens, looks forward to marrying Hippolyta, Queen of the Amazons. The marriage will take place in four days. Theseus orders Philostrate, his Master of Revels, to prepare the marriage celebration. Meanwhile, Egeus asks Theseus to punish his daughter Hermia for refusing to marry Demetrius, the man Egeus has chosen for her. Hermia prefers Lysander, whom she loves. Theseus reminds Hermia of her duty under Athenian law to obey her father or to suffer punishment: life as a nun, or death. To help her escape these harsh penalties, Lysander proposes that he and Hermia flee through nearby woods to a widowed aunt's house "seven leagues" (about 21 miles) away. There Athenian law does not apply. There he will marry her. She agrees.

Hermia tells her secret plan to Helena, her best friend. The latter loves Demetrius. To win favor with Demetrius, Helena plans to divulge Hermia's secret to him. Her reward will be the joy of seeing Demetrius return from the woods.

Summary (Scene 2) A group of Athenian laborers and tradesmen meet in the same woods to rehearse a play. They hope to perform this play for Theseus and Hippolyta on the night of the wedding. The play is about "the most cruel death of Pyramus and Thisby." Parts are assigned. Problems are discussed and possible solutions are offered.

READING COMPREHENSION

1. Why does Theseus feel that time is moving slowly? (Scene 1, line 3)

2. How does Hippolyta seek to soothe his impatience? (Scene 1, lines 7–11)

3. How can you tell Theseus was a warrior?

4. Often, early in a play or story, an unresolved problem is used to capture the interest of the reader or the audience. How is such a problem shown in Scene 1, lines 23–46?

5. In Scene 1, lines 23–46, Egeus accuses Lysander of foul actions in wooing Hermia. Cite six examples of these so-called foul actions. (Scene 1, lines 29–36)

6. We get a picture of the kind of control fathers exercised over daughters in Shakespeare's day. How is this shown? (Scene 1, lines 38, 42–46)

7. Cite evidence of Hermia's strong spirit. (Scene 1, lines 60–63)

8. Theseus shares the attitude of Egeus. How does he show this? (Scene 1, lines 47–53, 55–57)

9. What fate awaits a disobedient daughter? (Scene 1, lines 67–75)

10. Theseus contrasts the life of a nun with that of a woman who marries. What main points does he make in this contrast? (Scene 1, lines 71–80)

11. Is Theseus weak in yielding to Egeus' request? (Scene 1, lines 85–92) Explain.

12. Demetrius agrees with Egeus. Is this evidence that self-interest comes first with him? (Scene 1, lines 91, 92) Explain.

13. See Scene 1, lines 95–97. What qualities of Lysander do these words reveal?

14. What plan does Lysander suggest to Hermia so that they may get around her father's objections to him? (Scene 1, lines 158–170)

15. Why does Hermia agree to this plan? (Scene 1, lines 171–181)

16. Helena gives *six* reasons for envying Hermia. What are these reasons? (Scene 1, lines 186–196)

17. Some women inspire love even though they are cold to those who love them. How is this true of Hermia and Demetrius? (Scene 1, lines 199, 201, 203)

18. Why does Helena decide to tell Demetrius of her friends' secret plan? (Scene 1, lines 250–255)

19. Was Demetrius a dependable and constant lover? (Scene 1, lines 246–249) Explain.

20. Why is Quince having a meeting at his house? (Scene 2, lines 4–10)

21. Who will play Pyramus? (Scene 2, line 18)

22. How can you tell that Bottom is an enthusiastic actor? (Scene 2, lines 21–26)

23. Why does Flute object to playing a woman's part? (Scene 2, lines 43–44)

24. How does Quince refute (answer) Flute's objection? (Scene 2, lines 45–46)

25. How does Quince show he is in control? (Scene 2, lines 51–52)

26. Why does Snug want his part in writing? (Scene 2, line 62)

27. Why does Quince consider a script unnecessary for Snug? (Scene 2, line 64)

28. How does Bottom show once again his eagerness to participate? (Scene 2, lines 66–69)

29. Where and when will the rehearsal take place? (Scene 2, lines 93–96)

CHARACTERIZATION

Cite evidence that Theseus:

30. Likes entertainment. (Scene 1, lines 12–16)

31. Is an ex-warrior. (Scene 1, line 17)

32. Is respected. (Scene 1, line 21)

33. Tends to uphold the law. (Scene 1, lines 67, 85–92)

34. Is a busy man. (Scene 1, line 115)

Cite evidence that Hippolyta:

35. Is beautiful. (Scene 1, line 1)

36. Is patient. (Scene 1, lines 7–8)

Cite evidence that Egeus:

37. Is a dictatorial father. (Scene 1, lines 23–46)
38. Is unfair to Lysander. (Scene 1, lines 32, 37)

Cite evidence that Hermia:

39. Speaks up boldly. (Scene 1, lines 54–60)
40. Wants her own way. (Scene 1, line 58)
41. Is not frightened by threats. (Scene 1, line 81)
42. Is willing to act defiantly. (Scene 1, lines 171–181)
43. Is the type of young woman who exchanges confidences with a girlfriend. (Scene 1, lines 217–220)

Cite evidence that Lysander:

44. Has a sarcastic tongue. (Scene 1, line 96)
45. Can argue in his own behalf. (Scene 1, lines 101–112)
46. Is able to make plans to circumvent (get around) the law. (Scene 1, lines 159–170)

Cite evidence that Helena:

47. Is an envious person. (Scene 1, lines 184–196)
48. Is a persistent person. (Scene 1, line 202)
49. Has a low opinion of herself. (Scene 1, line 184)

50. Cite three instances to show that Bottom likes to take charge of what is going on. (Scene 2, lines 2–3, 8–10, 14–15)
51. How do we know that Bottom has a high opinion of his own acting ability? (Scene 2, lines 21–34)
52. Bottom is still ready to play every part. How does he show this? (Scene 2, line 66)
53. Bottom misuses words. Cite two examples. (Scene 2, lines 76, 101)
54. Where does Quince reject Bottom's suggestion? (Scene 2, lines 51–52)
55. See Scene 2, lines 76–78. Reading these lines, Bottom will demonstrate his skill in imitating bird sounds. Which birds will he imitate?

STYLE AND LANGUAGE

56. A *simile* is a direct comparison using "like," "as," or "than." Examples: cheeks like roses; red as a rose; hotter than the tropics in July. What simile do you find in Scene 1, lines 9–10?

57. To be emphatic, Shakespeare often resorts to listings. Thus, Egeus does more than merely accuse Lysander of giving gifts to Hermia. He specifies at least *eight* kinds of gifts. What are these *eight* gifts? (Scene 1, lines 29–35)

58. See Scene 1, line 37. Why is *filch'd* a better choice of word than any of these synonyms: stolen, pilfered purloined, lifted, pinched, snitched, swiped? (See Webster's *Dictionary of Synonyms* or a comparable source.)

59. See Scene 1, lines 130–133. *Metaphors* are *implied* comparisons. For example, a marble brow implies a brow as white as marble. What metaphors appear in these lines?

60. See Scene 1, lines 146–147. Point out three similes here.

61. See Scene 1, line 150. Point out the metaphor.

62. See Scene 1, lines 242–243. What metaphor is used here?

63. Classical allusions (references) are common in the speeches of Shakespeare's characters. Often these allusions add force and vigor to a character's expression of feeling.

   a. See Scene 1, line 173. Explain Cupid's "best arrow."

   b. See Scene 1, line 176. Explain "Carthage queen."

   c. See Scene 1, line 177. Explain "false Troyan."

64. See Scene 1, lines 198–210. Shakespeare uses "opposites" to invigorate his language. Give four examples of these opposites.

65. See Scene 1, lines 213–214. Point out two metaphors in these lines.

66. See Scene 1, lines 225–226. Explain the metaphor in these lines.

67. See Scene 1, line 233. Purist grammarians of today would correct a so-called error in grammar here. What correction would they make?

HUMAN RELATIONS

68. See Scene 1, lines 85–92 and 119–123. Is Theseus unduly harsh or is he merely upholding the customs of his day?

69. Some fathers in Shakespeare's day had the power and authority to select husbands for their daughters. In parts of our world today, marriages are arranged, thus depriving young people of their freedom of choice. What are the advantages and disadvantages of this practice? Explain why you would or would not favor a law forbidding this practice.

70. In Scene 1, line 48, Theseus says to Hermia: "To you your father should be as a god." Why do you agree or disagree with Theseus?

71. See Scene 1, lines 29–36.
  a. What picture of courting customs is presented here?
  b. Contrast this picture with contemporary (present-day) customs.

COMPARISONS WITH MODERN LIFE

72. Select any *one* of the statements below. Use it as a basis for comparing what happens in Act 1 with what you yourself have experienced or observed. Then develop the statement in a paragraph of about 100–150 words. Refer to the play. Be sure to include one or two specific examples.
  a. Now, as then, parents often find fault with the boyfriends or girlfriends of their children.
  b. Now, as then, children from time to time defy their parents' instructions or wishes.
  c. Now, as then, parents at times interfere with the social life or social preferences of their children.
  d. Now, as then, punishments are from time to time out of all proportion to the so-called offenses that are committed.
  e. Now, as then, "the course of true love never did run smooth."

SPEAK AND LISTEN: READING ALOUD

Oral interpretation (reading aloud) sharpens your apprecia-
tion of characterization, language, and the feelings conveyed
by words.

73. For reading aloud, select a speech at least eight lines long.
Make your choice for one or more of the reasons stated below.
   a. It is effectively vivid or descriptive.
   b. It is dramatic.
   c. It reflects the feelings of the speaker.
   d. It has thoughts worth remembering.
   e. It tells something special about the person speaking the
   lines.
   f. It illustrates a common problem in human relations.
   g. It shows the character facing a problem.
   h. It reminds us of similar problems today.
   i. It is worth selecting for some special reason not included
   in 1–8 above.

Summarize briefly the content of the speech.
Say why you selected the speech.
State one main objective you will have when you interpret
the speaker's words.
Practice reading the speech aloud. (If someone at home—
parent, brother, sister, friend—is willing to listen, fine. It's good
to practice with an audience.)
Be ready to read the speech to the class.
Finally, frame a question for the class based on this speech.
This question may call for explanation, interpretation, com-
ment, or opinion. It may even lead to controversy among your
classmates because of their differing views.

The SAMPLE ANSWER that follows will help guide you in preparing your response to this assignment:
   a. For reading aloud I have selected Act 1, lines 23–46.
   b. In this speech Egeus complains to Theseus that his daughter Hermia is disobedient. She wants to marry Lysander. Egeus
wants her to marry Demetrius. Egeus accuses Lysander of
having "filched" Hermia's love. He wants Theseus, applying
Athenian law, to punish her severely if she continues to dis-
obey her father.

c. I selected this speech for reasons a, b, c, e, f, g, and h.

d. My main objective is to portray Egeus' anger over Hermia's disobedience and over Lysander's actions.

e. My question for the class is the following: Considering the laws and the customs of Athens at the time of this speech, is daughter Hermia justified in acting as she does? Why or why not?

DRAMATIZATION

74. While the oral interpretation (reading aloud) of a single speech is a form of dramatization, think of dramatization under this heading as a performance by two or more students working together. The standards for selecting a portion of a play for dramatization can be similar to those listed under 73. In addition, however, there must be interaction between and among those acting. They can show contrasting emotions; for example, anger, joy, love, hate, fear, hope, suffering, despair. They can rebuke and insult each other. Or, as in Scene 2 of Act I, they can show humorously the attempt by simple people to plan a dramatic performance to entertain the Duke and his royal followers.

a. Select or elect a DIRECTOR to help plan dramatic presentations.

b. Let the DIRECTOR and his assistants assign parts, readers, actors.

c. Plan rehearsals.

d. Evaluate (judge) your rehearsals for ways of improving your performance.

e. Select a date for presenting your dramatization to the class.

f. Let the class evaluate the presentation through discussion. Emphasize mainly what members of the audience liked.

For example:

An actor's skill in projecting emotion
An actor's skill in portraying a character
An actor's ability to bring out the humor in a scene
The interaction between and among speakers

For Act I, consider among other possible selections, the following:

A daughter defies her father and the law. (Scene 1, lines 23–128)

Two young lovers fight despair. (Scene 1, lines 130–181)

Helena is envious. (Scene 1, lines 184–255)

The mechanics prepare to present a play. (Scene 2, lines 1–104)

Act II, Scenes 1 and 2

Summary (Scene 1)   Fairies, too, inhabit these nearby woods Here they carry out their midnight revels. Oberon, king of the fairies, wants as his page a little Indian prince (the changeling). Oberon's queen, Titania, has the boy. She promised the boy's mother she would take care of him. Also, she loves him as a son. Thus, she refuses to surrender him to Oberon. To torment Titania and to force her to give up the boy, Oberon instructs his mischievous servant Puck (or Robin Goodfellow) to obtain the juice of a purple flower called "love-in-idleness." This flower has been hit by Cupid's dart. Its juice on the eyes of a sleeping person can make that person fall in love with the first creature seen on awakening. Oberon hopes to squeeze the juice on Titania's eyes. He will then not lift the charm until she gives up the boy.

Demetrius, meanwhile, is in the woods looking for Lysander and Hermia. Although Helena has followed him, he rejects her. She says she loves him and will continue to pursue him.

Puck arrives with the magic flower. Taking it, Oberon plans to streak Titania's eyes with its juice. He orders Puck to use the juice on Demetrius to make the latter love Helena.

Summary (Scene 2)   Titania directs the fairies to perform various protective duties for her and then to sing her to sleep. Finding Titania asleep, Oberon squeezes the magic flower juice on her eyelids. Lysander and Hermia arrive. Tired, they fall asleep. Puck, who sees Lysander, mistakes the latter for Demetrius and squeezes the magic juice over Lysander's eyelids.

Helena, fleeing Demetrius, spots Lysander on the ground. Fearful he may be dead, she shakes him. He wakes up. Seeing Helena, he declares he loves her, not Hermia. Helena believes he is mocking and abusing her. She begs him to return to the sleeping Hermia. The latter, awakening from a bad dream, can't find Lysander. She proceeds to look for him.

READING COMPREHENSION

1. Puck reveals the fairy king's plans. What are they? (Scene 1, line 18)

2. See Scene 1, lines 19–26. Puck tells us that Oberon's queen, Titania, has as her attendant a changeling (stolen child), whom she loves. How does this make Oberon angry?

3. How does Titania make Oberon angry? (Scene 1, line 26)

4. What other name is used for Puck? (Scene 1, line 34)

5. Why are the milkmaids afraid of Puck? (Scene 1, lines 36, 37) (Also see facing page notes for line 36.)

6. See Scene 1, lines 39 and 47. Puck is responsible for two deceptions. What are they?

7. Check your dictionary for the definitions of *goblin* and *hobgoblin*. Then explain what qualities in Puck cause others to call him a Hobgoblin. (Scene 1, line 40)

8. What services does Puck perform for Oberon? (Scene 1, line 45)

9. See Scene 1, lines 52–55. What picture does Shakespeare give us in these lines?

10. See Scene 1, line 58. One can infer that Puck must be proud of a special ability he has. What is that ability?

11. There are at least five reasons why Oberon and Titania are quarreling. (Scene 1, lines 61–118)
  a. See Scene 1, lines 76–79. Theseus provides one reason for the quarreling. How?
  b. See Scene 1, line 63. What reason is given here?
  c. See Scene 1, lines 71–72, and facing page note. What reason is given here?
  d. See Scene 1 line 88. What reason is given here?

e. See Scene 1, lines 89–118 and the facing page notes for these lines. Here Titania blames Oberon for at least four kinds of bad luck. This bad luck, too, is a cause of quarreling. Mention the *four* ways in which Oberon's quarrels have brought bad luck.

12. How, according to Oberon, can Titania improve their relationship? (Scene 1, lines 121–122)

13. What is Titania's response to this request by Oberon? (Scene 1, lines 123–139)

14. What was the tragic fate of the changeling's mother? (Scene 1, line 137)

15. Why does Titania refuse to part with the changeling? (Scene 1, lines 138–139)

16. Not having his way, Oberon threatens Titania. What is this threat? (Scene 1, lines 148–149)

17. Oberon describes how Cupid's "bolt" fell upon a purple flower called "love-in-idleness." The juice of this flower has special properties. What are they? (Scene 1, lines 169–175)

18. How does Oberon plan to use this magic juice? (Scene 1, lines 180–182)

19. Why does he plan to do this? (Scene 1, line 189)

20. Why is Oberon able to overhear a conversation without being observed by others? (Scene 1, lines 190–191)

21. Helena pursues Demetrius. What is the latter's reaction to this pursuit? Why? (Scene 1, line 192)

22. Why is Demetrius in the woods? (Scene 1, lines 193–194)

23. Why does Helena compare herself to a dog? (Scene 1, lines 207–214)

24. Demetrius argues that Helena is in danger coming to the woods at night alone. How does Helena answer this argument? (Scene 1, lines 224–230)

25. See Scene 1, lines 249–250. What does Oberon plan to do?

26. See Scene 1, line 265. Who is the Athenian lady?

27. See Scene 1, line 266. Who is the disdainful youth?

28. Scene 2, lines 1–7 tell of *seven* activities carried on by fairies. What are they?

29. See Scene 2, lines 9–34. In songs and chorus there are detailed references to the world of nature, insects, and animals. Shakespeare refers to at least 12 living creatures. List these 12.

30. The fairies' songs aim to protect Titania. Why does she need protection? (Scene 2, lines 9–26)

31. See Scene 2, lines 27–34. What is Oberon doing? Why is he doing this?

32. See Scene 2, lines 39–65. What misunderstanding is at first apparent and then cleared up in these lines?

33. See Scene 2, lines 70, 71, 78, 79. What mischief does Puck perform?

34. See Scene 2, lines 84–87. What conflict is apparent here?

35. See Scene 2, lines 91–102. Cite evidence that Helena (a) envies Hermia and (b) has low self-esteem.

36. See Scene 2, line 103. How does this line show that Puck's magic has taken effect?

37. How does Helena try to protect her beloved Demetrius? (Scene 2, lines 108–110)

38. See Scene 2, lines 111–122. Lysander gives at least four explanations for preferring Helena to Hermia. What are they?

39. See Scene 2, lines 123–134. How does Helena see herself in these lines?

40. See Scene 2, lines 135–144. How do these lines reflect the power of Puck's sly work?

41. See Scene 2, lines 145–150. Why does Hermia "quake with fear"?

42. See Scene 2, line 156. Why does Hermia seem desperate?

CHARACTERIZATION

43. Scene 1, lines 1–15 tell you about Shakespeare's world of fairies. Two qualities of their movement are mentioned. What are they? (lines 6, 7)

44. Scene 1, lines 8–15 refer to three common activities or services performed by fairies. What are they?

45. Scene 1, lines 20 and 24 mention three qualities of Oberon. What are they?

46. See Scene 1, lines 65-69. Titania is finding fault with Oberon. Why?

47. See Scene 1, line 77. How does Oberon betray his jealousy?

48. See Scene 1, line 88. What characteristic of Oberon does Titania criticize?

49. See Scene 1, lines 152-156. From Oberon we learn four things about a mermaid. What are they?

50. See Scene 1, lines 192-232. On line 199 Helena calls Demetrius "hard-hearted." Cite at least *four* instances where his words justify this characterization.

51. Check *masochism* and *masochist* in your dictionary. Does Helena speak and act like a *masochist* during her exchange with Demetrius (Scene 1, lines 192-248)? Cite evidence to support your answer.

52. See Scene 2, lines 41-65. Compare with lines 103-144. The contrast illustrates fickleness of young love induced by the love potion. How does the contrast show this fickleness?

STYLE AND LANGUAGE

53. Part of Shakespeare's power comes from being specific and giving details. According to Titania, the quarrel between Oberon and her (Scene 1, lines 89-115) brought about at least *nine* disturbances in nature and on the land. List these *nine* disturbances in the order in which they are mentioned in lines 89-108.

54. See Scene 1, line 108. "The seasons alter."
   a. Cite three details as evidence of the alteration of the seasons. (lines 108-114)
   b. State one effect of this change on people. (line 115)

55. See Scene 1, lines 177-179. Why are the words *leviathan* and *girdle* used appropriately?

56. See Scene 1, lines 254-257. Shakespeare uses descriptive details to make a place seem real. In this instance, he depends on his intimate knowledge of flowers and plants. List *six* of these. Check each one in your dictionary. Tell briefly what your dictionary says about each one.

57. See Scene 1, line 260. Shakespeare uses a metaphor in this line. Explain the metaphor.

HUMAN RELATIONS

58. The Oberon-Titania relationship reflects a husband-wife conflict. They quarrel over custody of a child, but during their quarrel we observe anger, jealousy, threats, and accusations of infidelity.

On the basis of your own experience or your observation of others, what are some common causes of friction between husband and wife or between boyfriend and girlfriend? What, in your opinion, can contribute to an improved relationship? If you can do so, give specific examples.

59. See Scene 1, lines 245–246. Helena deplores the passive role of women in a courting relationship. Is there wisdom in maintaining this practice and tradition of a passive role for women being courted, or should it be replaced by a more active role for women, one consistent with modern ideas of women's liberation and equal rights for women? Explain.

COMPARISONS WITH MODERN LIFE

60. See Scene 1, lines 82–118. Titania is blaming natural disasters on Oberon's bad behavior. Are there parallel situations in modern life; for example, relating disaster to a curse, spite, witchcraft, an evil eye, astrology, one's date of birth, or some equally unscientific cause? Explain. If you can do so, give examples.

61. See Scene 1, lines 168–177. Here the juice of a flower has magical properties. Are there parallel situations in modern life where people believe in the special powers of potions, medicines, herbs, drugs, and extracts from plants? Explain. To what extent do you share these beliefs? Explain.

SPEAK AND LISTEN: READING ALOUD

Review item 73, Act I. (page 183) Pay special attention to the SAMPLE ANSWER, using it as your guide. Then, from Act II, select a speech at least eight lines long.

62. Following the instructions under 73, prepare in writing your guide for responding to this assignment.

For Act II consider, among other possible selections, the following:

Puck explains the Oberon-Titania quarrel. (Scene 1, lines 18–31)

Titania tells of disturbances in Nature. (Scene 1, lines 82–118)

Oberon enlists the help of Puck. (Scene 1, lines 253–273)

Lysander professes true love for Hermia. (Scene 2, lines 45–52)

Helena, running, envies Hermia and finds Lysander. (Scene 2, lines 88–102)

DRAMATIZATION

Review item 74, Act I. (page 184)

63. For Act II consider, among other possible selections, the following:

Oberon and Titania quarrel. (Scene 1, lines 61–149)

Oberon and Puck hatch a plot. (Scene 1, lines 150–191)

Demetrius repels Helena; she pursues him. (Scene 1, lines 192–250)

A victim of Puck's mischief, Lysander awakens to see Helena. Hermia awakens to find Lysander gone. (Scene 2, lines 103–56)

Act III, Scenes 1 and 2

Summary (Scene 1)　Again the laborers meet in the woods for a rehearsal. They revise the play to solve some problems they foresee. Puck listens. He then fastens a donkey's head upon Bottom. Titania, who has been sleeping nearby, awakens as Bottom sings. She loves his song. She loves him. She tells him he is "wise and beautiful." She promises she'll provide fairies to attend and serve him.

Summary (Scene 2)　In another part of the wood, Oberon gets a report from Puck. Puck reports that Titania has fallen in love with animal-headed Bottom. Both observe Demetrius professing to Hermia his love for her. The two argue. Hermia curses Demetrius, accusing him of slaying her beloved Lysander. She runs off to find Lysander. The latter falls asleep once more. At this point Oberon knows Puck has made a mistake. Oberon orders Puck to find Helena and to bring her near the sleeping Demetrius. Oberon says he'll charm Demetrius' eyes again before Helena appears—obviously to undo the mistake made by Puck. Puck fetches Helena. Meanwhile, Lysander and Helena appear together. Lysander continues to profess love to Helena. Awakening, Demetrius now sees Helena. The charm works. He is now madly in love with Helena. As Puck has predicted, now "two at once woo one." Helena suspects they are mocking her and that both really love Hermia. Lysander offers to surrender Hermia to Demetrius. The latter is not interested. Now he wants only Helena. The men argue, and Hermia appears. She is thoroughly confused by Lysander's change of affection. Helena now accuses all three of conspiring against her. Hermia is still confused. Arguments continue, with the lovers hurling bitter insults at each other.

Once again Oberon tries to mend things. He asks Puck to lead the two men in circles until they are weary. They will then fall asleep. Then Puck is to streak Lysander's eyes with a potion that will make everything seem like a dream and thus restore his love for Hermia. Oberon himself will see Titania, obtain the Indian boy, undo the charm, and release her from her passion for Bottom.

READING COMPREHENSION

1. See Scene 1, lines 8–11. What problem does Bottom foresee?

2. How do Snout and Starveling react to the problem that Bottom foresees? (Scene 1, lines 12–14)

3. How does Bottom propose to solve this problem? (Scene 1, lines 15–21)

4. What problem does Snout foresee? (Scene 1, line 26)

5. While Snout suggests another prologue to avoid this problem, Bottom has a different idea. What is Bottom's solution? (Scene 1, lines 34–43)

6. There are two suggestions for showing moonlight. What are they? (Scene 1, lines 51–56)

7. Two new characters are added to the play. Who are they? (Scene 1, lines 54–56, 61)

8. Pyramus and Thisby are to whisper to each other through an opening in a wall. Bottom explains how to represent this opening. What does he suggest? (Scene 1, lines 61–65)

9. Who begins the rehearsal? (Scene 1, lines 66–67, 75)

10. Who, unobserved by the others, listens to the rehearsal? (Scene 1, lines 71–74)

11. Bottom misuses words. Give an example. (Scene 1, line 76)

12. Who corrects him? (Scene 1, line 77)

13. See Scene 1, line 108. Snout says to Bottom, ". . . thou art changed!" What change does Snout see?

14. Why does Bottom sing? (Scene 1, lines 115–116)

15. What effect does his singing have upon Titania? (Scene 1, line 121)

16. How does Titania respond to Bottom's song? (Scene 1, lines 130–134)

17. See Scene 1, lines 136–137. What evidence do we have so far in the play that "reason and love keep little company together"? Give at least three examples.

18. See Scene 1, line 140. Why is Puck partly responsible for Titania's speaking this way?

19. Titania promises at least *four* rewards to Bottom if he stays with her in the forest. What will these rewards be? (Scene 1, lines 148–152)

20. Who are the fairy servants ready to attend upon Bottom? (Scene 1, line 153)

21. Titania wants the fairy servants to treat Bottom well. Mention at least two of the ways in which they will serve him. (Scene 1, lines 159–166)

22. See Scene 2, lines 4–35. Puck tells how he put an animal head on Bottom (line 18). What effect upon the other actors resulted from their seeing this costume? (Scene 2, line 25)

23. See Scene 2, line 36. Why is Oberon pleased?

24. Why is Demetrius displeased with Hermia? (Scene 2, lines 44–45)

25. See Scene 2, lines 48–58. In the absence of Lysander, what does Hermia suspect?

26. See Scene 2, lines 59–62. Why does Demetrius call Hermia a murderer?

27. Hermia's immediate reply to this accusation shows that she is not interested in Demetrius. How does she show this? (Scene 2, lines 63–64)

28. See Scene 2, line 65. What feeling toward Lysander does Demetrius express here?

29. Where does Hermia show that she has a sharp tongue? Cite the lines.

30. Why doesn't Demetrius follow Hermia when she leaves him? (Scene 2, line 83)

31. How does Oberon see Helena? (Scene 2, line 97)

32. See Scene 2, line 119. Who are the "two"?

33. Who is the "one"? (Scene 2, line 119)

34. See Scene 2, lines 120–122. How do these lines show Puck's impish nature?

35. See Scene 2, lines 123–128. How does Lysander try to prove his love for Helena is genuine?

36. See Scene 2, lines 129–134. Helena argues that Lysander has made the same vows to Hermia. What conclusion does she draw from that fact?

37. See Scene 2, lines 135 and 137. Lysander argues he lacked judgment when he wooed Hermia. He says Demetrius loves Hermia and not Helena. How do the first words of Demetrius, awakening, prove Lysander is wrong?

38. See Scene 2, lines 146–162. Where is Helena being sarcastic?

39. Helena says Lysander and Demetrius are uncivilized and discourteous. She says their praise of her is mere mockery. Why does she not believe them? (Scene 2, lines 146–162)

40. Lysander is now willing to surrender to Demetrius his former interest in Hermia. Why? (Scene 2, line 166)

41. How does Demetrius respond to Lysander's offer to surrender Hermia? (Scene 2, lines 170–174)

42. What effect does darkness have upon the senses? (Scene 2, line 179)

43. See Scene 2, lines 188–192. Why did Lysander leave Hermia?

44. See Scene 2, lines 194–221. Helena scolds Hermia. Why?

45. Helena gives *four* reasons why Hermia should be more loyal to Helena. What are these reasons? (Scene 2, lines 200–221)

46. See Scene 2, lines 222–223. How does Hermia respond to Helena's scolding her?

47. See Scene 2, lines 224–237. Apparently both Lysander and Demetrius have been praising Helena and speaking words of love to her? Why does Helena not believe them?

48. How does Hermia react to Helena's accusation? (Scene 2, line 238)

49. See Scene 2, lines 239–242. Helena believes Hermia is part of a plot to make fun of her. How can we tell?

50. Lysander professes love for Helena. (Scene 2, line 248) Even Hermia suspects a scornful Lysander. (line 249) Demetrius, too, swears love for Helena. (line 257) What effect does all this have upon Hermia? (line 260)

51. Where does Lysander rudely insult Hermia? (Scene 2, line 261)

52. Where does Lysander rudely insult Demetrius? (Scene 2, line 265)

53. Why does Lysander call Hermia "a tawny Tartar"? (Scene 2, line 269) (Check each word in your dictionary.)

54. See Scene 2, lines 277 and 285–289. How do these lines reflect the fickleness of young love?

55. See Scene 2, line 290. To whom does Hermia address these words?

56. See Scene 2, line 298. Why is Hermia so upset when Helena calls her a "puppet"?

57. See Scene 2, line 312. How can we tell that Helena fears Hermia will assault her?

58. See Scene 2, lines 316–327. Cite evidence that Helena wants to remain on good terms with Hermia.

59. See Scene 2, line 359. Hermia is still completely confused. How can we tell?

60. Oberon blames Puck for the confusion. Is Puck sorry for the mischief he has caused? (Scene 2, lines 360–361)

61. See Scene 2, lines 369–381. Oberon gives detailed instructions to Puck. Puck is to do at least *eight* things.
  a. See line 369. What is the first of these?
  b. See lines 370–372. What is the second?
  c. See line 373. What is the third?
  d. See line 375. What is the fourth?
  e. See line 376. What is the fifth?
  f. See line 377. What is the sixth?
  g. See line 379. What is the seventh?
  h. See line 381. What is the eighth?

62. See Scene 2, lines 391–392. What will Oberon do on his own to reverse the damage he has done?

63. Puck urges hasty action. (Scene 2, lines 393–397) Why must Oberon's plan be carried out without delay?

64. Why is Oberon not upset by Puck's plea for haste? (Scene 2, lines 403–408)

65. See Scene 2, lines 411–449. In these lines Puck is carrying out the mischief required by Oberon's instructions in lines 369–381.
  a. See lines 411–414. What mischief is suggested here?
  b. See lines 416–417. Also, see line 377. What inference can you make regarding Puck's words here?
  c. See lines 419–420. Also, see lines 373–374. What is Puck up to?
  d. See lines 424–428. Also, see lines 375–376. What mischief is Puck performing here?

66. See Scene 2, lines 438, 449, 455, 466. What condition now overcomes the four lovers?

67. See Scene 2, lines 467–482. How has Puck carried out Oberon's instructions?

STYLE AND LANGUAGE

68. When the mechanicals (laborers and tradesmen) meet for the play rehearsal (Scene 1, lines 1–99), their conversation is in ordinary prose. When other characters speak, we hear poetry. What is Shakespeare's purpose in creating this difference in speech patterns?

69. See Scene 1, lines 136–137. Bottom may be a lower class laborer, but at times Shakespeare allows him to speak words of wisdom. Cite an example here. Then explain what Bottom means.

70. See Scene 1, lines 159–169. Here Titania is trying to make Bottom's new life with her very attractive and pleasant for him. To convey a sense of this attractiveness, Shakespeare gives us a list of the services that will be performed for him. Cite *five* of these.

See Scene 2, line 141. Demetrius refers to Helena's lips as "kissing cherries."

71. Why is this a metaphor?

72. Why is it an appropriate metaphor?

73. See Scene 2, lines 205–216. What figure of speech do we find here? Why is it appropriate?

74. Shakespeare is masterful in selecting epithets (disparaging or abusive words or phrases) for his characters to hurl at one another, especially when they are quarreling and angry. For each example below, cite the epithet. Then, unless it is obvious, tell why the epithet is supposed to hurt the person at whom it is directed. Use your dictionary for *Ethiope, burr, tawny, Tartar, juggler, counterfeit, puppet, maypole.*

Check all meanings given. These will give you clues for interpreting each epithet.

  a. See line 261.

b. See lines 265–266.
c. See line 269.
d. See line 290.
e. See line 297.
f. See line 298.
g. See line 305.

CHARACTERIZATION

During rehearsal in Scene 1, Bottom foresees several problems. For each one he offers a solution. If Pyramus' suicide by sword will offend the ladies, he suggests a prologue to dispel such fear. If a lion will frighten the ladies, he wants the audience to see the actor's face through the lion's neck. If the moon must shine, Bottom calls for an almanac to find out whether the moon will be shining on the night of the play. If a wall is necessary, an actor must play Wall.

Yet Puck (Scene 2, line 14) calls Bottom a "shallow thickskin."

Some actors take Bottom for an ass and consider the donkey head he wears as Shakespeare's symbolic representation of Bottom's character. Others see him as a delightful, ingenious, cooperative, enthusiastic individual with virtues outweighing faults.

75. What is your assessment of Bottom? Why do you feel this way? Refer to what he says in the play and to what others say about him to support your point of view.

If you were playing Bottom, would you want the audience to respect you, laugh at you, or do both? Why?

76. In the preceding question you have seen how an assessment of a character in a play can be controversial.

Think of a controversial person you know. Regarding this person, you and possibly others have mixed feelings. This person can be a friend, acquaintance, brother, sister, mother, father, relative, boyfriend, girlfriend, or someone you have read about or watched on the screen (movies or TV).

a. Describe this person.
b. Summarize his or her virtues.

c. Summarize his or her faults.

d. Give one or two examples of your experience with this person that made a strong impression on you one way or another.

e. Then give your final judgment of this person, saying whether and why your overall reaction is favorable, unfavorable, or mixed.

COMPARISONS WITH MODERN LIFE

77. In Act III you have observed how Puck's mischief caused misunderstanding and confusion. Puck and his magic juice were mostly to blame. In our own lives, however, similar problems often result from causes that are very real.

Think of an experience you have had where misunderstanding or confusion has been the result of a mistake or where it has some other cause.

a. Describe the misunderstanding or confusion.

b. Tell what happened to create it.

c. Tell whether anything happened to make things even worse than they should have been.

d. Were the problems ever cleared up? If so, how? Give details. If not, why not?

e. What could be done in the future to prevent similar misunderstanding or confusion?

78. This is an *optional* written assignment for those wishing to experiment with creative writing.

In Act III you have observed how friends quarrel, abuse each other with vile name-calling, accuse each other, show distrust, and suffer hurt feelings. Think of such a quarrel between two people in which you have been a participant or of a quarrel you have observed. Using dialog, write the scene that takes place between two quarreling people.

SPEAK AND LISTEN: READING ALOUD

Review item 73, Act I. (page 183) Then, from Act III, select a speech at least eight lines long.

79. Following the instructions under 73 on page 183, prepare in writing your guide for responding to this assignment.

For Act III consider, among other possible selections, the following:

Titania shows love for Bottom (Scene 1, lines 143–152)
Titania asks the elves to show courtesies to Bottom (Scene 1, lines 153–169)
Puck reports to Oberon on Titania's new love (Scene 2, lines 7–35)
Helena reacts when she suspects her friends are mocking her (Scene 2, lines 146–162)
Hermia reacts when Helena calls her a puppet (Scene 2, lines 298–307)

DRAMATIZATION

Review item 74, Act I. (page 184)
80. For Act III consider, among other possible selections, the following:

The mechanicals (laborers) rehearse (Scene 1, line 99)
Hermia and Demetrius quarrel (Scene 2, lines 42–88)
The four lovers quarrel (Scene 2, lines 123–346)

Act IV, Scenes 1 and 2

Summary (Scene 1) Titania still loves Bottom. She strokes his cheeks, sticks roses in his head, and kisses his large donkey ears. Bottom enjoys many luxuries. Oberon welcomes Puck. Oberon tells of his taunting Titania for loving Bottom. Now that Oberon has the boy, he restores Titania to her normal state.

Theseus, Hippolyta, and Egeus are in the woods to watch Theseus' hounds in the hunt. Egeus finds the four young lovers asleep. Theseus has the huntsmen awaken them with their horns. Theseus is surprised to find them so peacefully together.

Egeus persists in wanting to punish his daughter. Theseus, noting the new harmony among the couples, overrules Egeus' plea. Theseus will set aside the hunting plans and invite the couples to join the marriage festivities in Athens.

Awakening, Bottom remembers his strange dream.

Summary (Scene 2) At Quince's house in Athens, Bottom rejoins his fellow players. They are happy to see him. He instructs them regarding the specific preparations each one must make to be ready for the play.

READING COMPREHENSION

1. Titania is in love with a donkey-faced Bottom. How can you tell? (Scene 1, lines 1–4)

2. The fairy servants are ready to grant Bottom every whim and wish. Cite evidence of this fact. (Scene 1, lines 7–26)

3. Even Titania heeds his wishes. Cite *two* examples of what she is ready to do. (Scene 1, lines 27–33)

4. What food is available for Bottom? (Scene 1, lines 35–36)

5. Cite evidence that Titania is in love with Bottom. (Scene 1, lines 39–44)

6. Oberon begins to feel sorry for Titania. He has scolded her for crowning Bottom's head with fresh flowers. Why is Oberon ready to "undo the hateful imperfection" of Titania's eyes—that is, to restore her to her normal state? (Scene 1, lines 56–62)

7. What does Oberon ask Puck to do? (Scene 1, lines 63–64, 80)

8. See Scene 1, lines 74–76. Waking up, Titania thinks she has been dreaming. What was her dream?

9. See Scene 1, line 80. Who removes the donkey head?

10. See Scene 1, lines 87–92. Oberon and Titania are now on good terms again. What do they look forward to?

11. Theseus is out hunting. How can you tell? (Scene 1, lines 103, 106–108)

12. How can you tell that Hippolyta enjoys the sport of hunting? (Scene 1, lines 112–118)

13. Egeus finds the four lovers fast asleep. (Scene 1, lines 128–131) How does Theseus explain their presence in the woods? (lines 132–134)

14. Who orders that the sleeping lovers be awakened? (Scene 1, line 138)

15. Why is Theseus surprised by what he observes? (Scene 1, lines 142–146)

16. How does Lysander explain why all four are so peacefully together? (Scene 1, lines 147–154)

17. How does Egeus react to Lysander's confession? (Scene 1, lines 155–160)

18. Demetrius confesses Helena's role in bringing him to the wood. He says he no longer loves Hermia. Cite evidence that he now loves only Helena. (Scene 1, lines 171–172, 178)

19. What happens to the plan for the day's hunting? (Scene 1, line 184)

20. How many people will celebrate marriages in Athens? (Scene 1, line 185)

21. The four lovers wake up, not sure whether they are awake or still asleep and dreaming. They follow Theseus, Hippolyta, and Egeus to the temple. (Scene 1, lines 188–201) How does the scene end? (lines 204–222)

22. Quince can't find Bottom. How does Starveling explain Bottom's absence? (Scene 2, lines 1–4)

23. Why is Quince upset to find Bottom absent? (Scene 2, lines 7, 8)

24. Flute, too, is worried about Bottom's absence. Why? (Scene 2, line 20)

25. Bottom will not talk about himself. He thinks only of the play. He asks the other actors to get ready. What *six* things must they do to prepare for the play? (Scene 2, lines 31–42)

CHARACTERIZATION

26. See Scene 1, line 48. What is Oberon's opinion of Bottom?

27. See Scene 1, lines 56–62. What evidence do we have that

Titania succumbs to taunts (sarcastic challenges or insults)?

28. See Scene 1, line 180. Cite evidence that Theseus is flexible in applying Athenian law.

29. See Scene 2, lines 5–14. The actors in the Pyramus and Thisby play give their opinions of Bottom. Summarize what they say about him.

30. See Scene 2, lines 31–42. Cite evidence that Bottom is efficient in helping the others prepare for the play.

31. *For Creative Writers:* See Scene 1, lines 1–44. Bottom is enjoying the rare luxury of having, for the moment, an ideal and luxurious existence. Although he wears a donkey head, he is like a king (while Queen Titania is in love with him).

Imagine yourself having a choice and being able to command a routine for one day that you would consider ideal—the fulfillment of a dream. Describe this ideal day. (Give as much detail as Shakespeare does in describing Bottom's life of being served and of having anything he wants.) Write about 150 words.

STYLE AND LANGUAGE

32. See Scene 1, lines 41–44. What comparison reinforces the picture of Titania's embracing Bottom?

33. See Scene 1, line 62. To what does Oberon refer when he speaks of "the hateful imperfection" of Titania's eyes?

34. See Scene 2, lines 12–14. How does Quince misuse a word?

HUMAN RELATIONS

35. Early in the play Theseus supports Egeus. He upholds Athenian law. Later (Scene 1, line 180) he relents, overruling his earlier decision and negating his own Athenian law. Explain why you approve or disapprove of his second decision.

36. See Scene 1, line 144. The "gentle concord" follows a night of bitter enmity, turmoil, quarrels, and confusion. The best explanation (see line 203) when the confusion ends is that it was a night of dreams.

a. Think of a time when you had a confusing and disturbing dream, perhaps one involving enmity and quarrels. Describe it.

b. Tell whether there was any connection between the dream and reality.

c. Tell how you reacted when you realized you had been dreaming.

37. Think of a person you know who is dedicated, as Theseus was to hunting, to a sport or another favorite activity. Give an example of this dedication.

Tell what happens when this person faces a conflict between this favorite activity and another one—possibly a duty or obligation that is less attractive to the person. How does this person resolve the problem? Tell whether the resolution is one that you admire—and why.

COMPARISON WITH MODERN LIFE

38. Write a paragraph of about 100–150 words developing any *one* of the statements below:

a. Now, as then, those preparing to put on a play face many problems requiring ingenious or creative solutions.

b. Now, as then, the course of true love never runs smooth.

c. Now, as then, reason and good judgment are not the main ingredients of a relationship between young lovers.

d. Now, as then, reality is often better than one's dreams.

e. Now, as then, people dream of getting the kind of service and attention Bottom had when Titania fell in love with him.

f. Now, as then, a group misses a good person when this person seems to be unavailable.

SPEAK AND LISTEN: READING ALOUD

Review item 73, Act I. (page 183) Then, from Act IV, select a speech at least eight lines long.

39. Following the instructions under 73, prepare in writing your guide for responding to this assignment.

For Act IV consider, among other possible selections, the following:

Oberon observes the "imperfection of Titania's eyes."
(Scene 1, lines 45–74)
Theseus prepares to go hunting. (Scene 1, lines 103–111)
Bottom awakens from his dream. (Scene 1, lines 204–222)

DRAMATIZATION

Review item 74, Act I. (page 184)
40. For Act IV consider, among other possible selections, the following:

Bottom enjoys the good life. (Scene 1, lines 1–44)
Egeus and Theseus find the lovers. (Scene 1, lines 128–187)
The actors miss Bottom—and then find him. (Scene 2, lines 1–42)

Act V

Summary In the palace of Theseus in Athens, the Duke and his followers await the evening's entertainment.

Of several choices offered by Philostrate, Duke Theseus selects Pyramus and Thisby because he values the simplicity and sense of duty that characterized the preparation for the performance. The play amuses some and bores others.

At the end of the play, Bottom asks whether the Duke would like an epilogue or a country dance. No epilogue is needed, says the Duke, since all of the players are now dead. He prefers the country dance. He then announces a fortnight (14 days) of "nightly revels" and "jollity."

Puck cleans house for the fairy king and queen. The fairies sing and dance. Oberon blesses the marrying couples and predicts healthy children.

Puck apologizes to the audience. To escape hisses from the

audience, he promises to "make amends ere long." To make up for all the defects in the play, he promises to improve the play.

READING COMPREHENSION

1. Why does Theseus put lunatics, lovers, and poets in the same category? (lines 2–22)

2. Hippolyta thinks the night's events show more than just ideas created by the imagination. What impresses her the most? (lines 23–27)

3. What does Theseus look forward to? (lines 33–43)

4. Why does Theseus call for Philostrate? (lines 39–45)

5. What are the first three choices Philostrate offers? (lines 46–60)

6. Philostrate's last choice is the Pyramus and Thisby performance. What is Philostrate's opinion of this play? (lines 63–84)

7. Why does Theseus, overruling Philostrate, say he wants to hear the play? (lines 85–87)

8. Who says it is not enough to speak, but that one must speak accurately? (lines 124–125)

9. Who agrees with Lysander? (lines 126–127)

10. Quince speaks the prologue. It stresses the good will of the actors. They come to delight the audience. What fault does Theseus find in Quince's recitation of the prologue? (lines 122–129)

11. In the prologue, Quince presents Pyramus, Thisby, Wall, Moonshine, and Lion. He then summarizes the plot. In the moonlight Pyramus and Thisby meet at Ninus' tomb to woo. A lion scares Thisby who, fleeing, drops her mantle. The lion stains her mantle with blood. What, then, happens to Pyramus and Thisby? (lines 130–154)

12. How can we tell the lion arouses the curiosity of Theseus? (line 155)

13. Demetrius refers to "many asses." To whom is he referring? (line 156)

14. Snout plays the Wall. What purpose does the Wall serve? (lines 160–166)

15. See lines 179–187. The stones of the wall deceive Pyramus because they prevent him from seeing Thisby. But the words "deceiving me" have a special significance for Thisby. What is that significance?

16. See line 202. Why is the audience likely to laugh at this point?

17. See line 210. What is Hippolyta's opinion of the play?

18. See line 216. Theseus continues to accept the play as entertainment. What, according to him, must the audience do?

19. Why does Theseus call the lion "a very gentle beast"? (line 225)

20. Which members of the audience praise Lion, Thisby, and Moon? (lines 257–260)

21. See lines 263–299. Pyramus, having chased the lion away, finds Thisby's mantle stained with blood (line 275). What action does he take as a consequence of this discovery? (lines 289–299)

22. Puns figure in the reactions of Demetrius, Lysander, and Theseus. What does this show of the nature of their response to the tragedy on the stage? (lines 300–304)

23. How can you tell that Hippolyta is getting impatient? (lines 308–309)

24. See lines 315–338. Thisby, finding Pyramus dead, reacts violently. What does she do?

25. Bottom offers the audience a choice—an epilogue or a country dance. How does Theseus respond to this offer? (lines 342–351)

26. Where does Theseus refer to the play as stupid? (line 356)

27. How long will the celebration go on? (line 358)

28. See lines 360–379. Puck's speech stresses the special activities and qualities of the world of darkness. What are they? (Mention at least *seven*.)

29. See lines 380–411. Oberon and Titania lead the fairies in song and dance. Oberon offers a special blessing for the loving couples. What hopes and good wishes does he extend?

30. See lines 412–427. Puck's last speech is an apology. What does he apologize for?

31. How does Puck hope to escape hisses from the audience? (line 427)

CHARACTERIZATION

32. See lines 28–30. How do these lines show the wholesome character and kindly nature of Theseus?

33. See lines 33–43. Cite evidence of Theseus' love of entertainment.

34. See lines 73–88. How does Theseus show his sympathy for the lower classes and for simple people?

35. Who prefers "tongue-tied simplicity" to "audacious eloquence"? (lines 105–109)

36. See lines 246–248. How does Theseus show his good manners?

37. See lines 308–309. How does Hippolyta reveal her nature here?

STYLE AND LANGUAGE

38. See lines 7, 8. These lines are frequently quoted. Why?

39. See lines 126–127. Why is the comparison appropriate?

40. See lines 128–129. Why is the comparison appropriate?

41. See lines 149–150, 152. *Alliteration* is the repetition of initial consonant sounds. It's a common language device for emphasis and sometimes for comic effects. Shakespeare uses this device here. Cite three examples.

42. Shakespeare uses blunders involving names as a source of humor. Explain the blunder in lines 197 and 198.

43. Puck wants to escape "the serpent's tongue." This is a metaphor for hisses from the audience. Why is the metaphor (the implied comparison) appropriate? (line 422)

HUMAN RELATIONS

44. People in authority are often disliked, especially when their rule is cold, arbitrary, and unjust. Theseus, apparently, is well-liked and respected.

Using evidence from the play, especially in Act V, explain why this is true. Cite examples to support your conclusion.

COMPARISONS WITH MODERN LIFE

45. See lines 398–403. Oberon is hoping that the loving couples will bear children free from birth defects.

a. He mentions four birth defects apparently common in Shakespeare's day. What are they?

b. These birth defects occur even today. However, at least *two* other defects are serious problems today. Name them.

c. Several defects not mentioned by Oberon were known in Shakespeare's day and occur today. Name as many as you can.

46. Write a paragraph of 100–150 words on one of the following topics.

a. Now, as then, the fate of actors depends on the audience.

b. Now, as then, people seek entertainment between dinner-time and bedtime.

c. Now, as then, some stage or movie performances frighten some members of the audience.

d. Now, as then, the response of individual members of an audience varies greatly.

SPEAK AND LISTEN: READING ALOUD

Review item 73, Act I. (page 183) Then, from Act V, select a speech at least eight lines long.

47. Following the instructions under 73, prepare in writing your guide for responding to this assignment.

For Act V consider, among other possible selections, the following:

Theseus discourses on lovers, madmen, and poets. (lines 2–22)
Snout explains his role as Wall. (lines 157–166)
Pyramus talks to the wall. (lines 170–181)
The lion introduces himself. (lines 217–224)
Pyramus kills himself. (lines 283–299)
Thisby kills herself. (lines 315–338)
Puck concludes the play. (lines 360–379)

DRAMATIZATION

Review item 74, Act I. (page 184)
48. For Act V consider, among other possible selections, the
following:

Theseus greets the lovers and prepares to see the play.
   (lines 1–109)
The laborers and tradesmen present Pyramus and Thisby.
   (lines 112–338)